I Know W[hy the] Manatee Swims Naked

I've Shopped for Bathing Suits, Too

Rebel Lowrey Covan

I Know Why the Manatee Swims Naked

I've Shopped for Bathing Suits, Too

by **Rebel Lowrey Covan**

ISBN: 0-9702140-0-6

Original Artwork by:
Chelsea Covan

Printed in the United States of America
Fourth Printing January 2002

Published by **Dockside Publications, Inc.**
Pensacola, FL
(850) 479-3305

ACKNOWLEDGMENTS

Anyone who has ever written a book knows that it is never a one-person job. Even though the words in this book are mine, they would never have made their way to print without the efforts, encouragement, and sacrifice of a great many people (some of whom I am bound to omit, and whose forgiveness I humbly seek).

First of all, to my loving and precious Heavenly Father: Thank You so very, very much for blessing me with the treasured gift of being able to help people smile.

To my wonderful husband, Les (a/k/a "That Poor, Poor Man"): Thank you for your love and support. Thank you for being the good-natured subject of so much of my writing, and for bearing it all with a tremendous sense of humor. I love you truly.

To my precious first-born, Carly: Thank you for letting Mom share with so many people the zoo that is our home – and our relationship. You are so beautiful and funny, how could I *not* write about you? I love you madly.

To my precious last-born, Chelsea: Thank you for the hysterical manatee drawings. You are so talented, and gorgeous, *and* hilarious! And thanks for providing "comical fodder" for this book. I love you deeply.

To my editor/publisher and best friend, Lyn Zittel: Thanks for laughing and encouraging and supporting and (yes, even) nagging! If it weren't for you, this book wouldn't be. Thanks for saying to so many *Dockside* readers, "You look like you could use a good laugh, read page five first!" You're the kind of person I wish every woman could have as a best friend. I love you like a sister.

To my wonderful friend and great giggler, Judi Mixson: Thanks for proofing and editing and laughing, and for all the encouraging words "lo" these many years. I love you, too.

To my dear friend and talented painter of words, Roselyn Stone: Thank you for believing in me and for giving me the first "outlet" for my written words. I love you, also.

To my precious Aunt Linnie (Pooh Pooh) Magon: Thanks for keeping *Dockside* in your bathroom library! I love you oh-so much!

To my darling Aunt Minnie (Moo Moo) Austin: Thank you for your prayers and for being the spiritual cornerstone of our family. I love you very much!

DEDICATION

This book is dedicated to

my wonderful mom,

Winnie Rosella Levens Foley Lowrey Rotch

(a/k/a "BoBo"),

and to the memory of my

precious little "Mamaw,"

Addie Belle Whitfield Levens.

Table of Contents

MISS ELAINE-E-OUS *(continued)*

FOURTEEN YEARS OF TERRIBLE TWO'S

TV OR NOT TV?

SOUTHERNISMS

HOLIDAYS: BRIBERY, GRINCHES & A THERMOS OF GRITS

FEELING "FLAB-ULOUS!"

THE GREAT SPANDEX CHALLENGE

It's too late. It's summer already. I finally figured out that there's probably no way in the world I can lose 35 pounds and firm up my thunder thighs and underarm dingle-dangle by next week. And since I'm 50, I'd feel (and, no doubt, *look*) pretty silly wearing that maternity bathing suit I've held on to for sentimental reasons for the past 14 years.

And last year's bathing suits . . . well, they've all paid their dues. They richly deserve retirement. They worked really hard for me last summer. They stretched and cinched with the best of them. The "tummy minimizer" maxed out. The "thigh minimizer" gave my thighs a really good run for their money, but lost. And the "torso lengthener" just couldn't compete with the accordion that is my midsection. But what a valiant effort they all made. I'm convinced that man (or whoever) will probably never be able to create spandex strong enough to take on my body.

But, masochist that I am, I never give up hope. So last week, I went bathing suit shopping — that great sinkhole for those of us who feel there's not enough in this world to depress us.

There I was, surrounded by bathing suits of every style and color imaginable — among them, blacks (that great fat camouflager), florals (what a slenderizing effect *those* have on the large body), and oranges ("The Great Pumpkin Swims").

And, of course (just to add a further twist of the knife), the salesperson that "helped" me is young enough to be my daughter and small enough to be my leg.

"Oh, now, I know you're not looking forward to this," she assumed correctly, "but I've helped a lot of older women even fatter than you are. We're going to make this, like, a totally pleasant experience! I've been specially trained to find just the right suit to correct all those figure flaws of yours!"

And I distinctly remember thinking, "You know, I could sit on you, and no one would find you for weeks."

"So, what size suit will we be needing?" she asked.

"No idea," I responded truthfully.

"Well, then, what *dress* size are we?" asked the little Poster Girl for the Tactfully-Challenged.

"*We* are probably about a 16, together; but I, myself, am . . . usually a size 8; but I'm retaining a little water this week, so maybe you'd better bring me a 14."

"A 14 *dress*? Well, if you normally wear a size 14 dress, then you're going to need *at least* a size 20 bathing suit," the wee one informed me as she left in search of the perfect suit.

She came back in a relatively short time, considering her mission, armed with what appeared to be about 30 bathing suits. Actually, there were only six — mostly florals.

"Will you be needing any help getting into these?"

"No thanks. I brought some Pam®."

She didn't get it. But, thankfully, she did leave me in peace — or at least alone.

Two hours later, spandex burns covering my body, I walked out of the fitting room — a depleted and defeated woman. I fought the suits, and the suits won. There was no one and nothing on earth that could make me admit to that little Twiggy of a salesclerk that this experience made me understand why manatees swim naked.

"Thanks for all your help," I said as I returned the suits, "but I just couldn't find anything that I really liked all that much."

"Well, I hope you won't take this the wrong way," she said, "but our Maternity Department carries quite an extensive (good thing for her she didn't say 'wide') selection of suits for women of your . . . uh . . . proportions."

Why couldn't she have just said, "Thank you very much for shopping with us. I'm sorry we couldn't help you. Here's your Prozac®."

D-I-E-T IS A FOUR-LETTER WORD

I was a child whose skinny, little legs made all the shorts I wore look like bell-bottoms; a teenager who ate peanut butter-and-banana sandwiches and drank milkshakes four times a day in order to gain weight; and a college student who was once told, "Excuse me, but you have a couple of long threads hanging from your skirt. Oh, I'm sorry — those are your *legs*!" I never in my wildest nightmares (before I turned 30) dreamt that I'd ever have to resort to that most profane of four-letter words: "D-I-E-T." Oh, of course, there was that "settling" of fat molecules that occurred when I was 23. And that pre-middle-aged spread that set in when I turned 30. But nobody ever told me how hard it was to lose "baby fat." I'm not referring to the kind you get when you're 18 months old that sort of hangs around until you're six. I'm talking about the kind that comes along when you're six months pregnant with your first baby.

Not that I'm naïve, but I had just assumed that since Cher had a displayable belly button within seven hours after Chastity was born, so would I after Carly was born. Well, in the first place, no one even bothered to inform me that my belly button would go from an "inny" to an "outy" by the fifth month of my pregnancy. That was a totally rude awakening for me. Unfortunately, I was pregnant during the early '80s, when gossamer-type maternity outfits were *en vogue*. As a result, I had to resort to wearing tape over my protruding belly button. I had just naturally presupposed, as well, that my belly button would go concave immediately upon Carly's birth. Wrong, as well. In addition to awakening from general anesthesia flat on my back to view a belly that, rather than looking anything like Cher's, looked like my obstetrician just might have forgotten to take out my baby's twin, I still had a projectile belly button.

I'd seen supermodels, movie stars, singers, and women television personalities bounce back from baby fat in a time period that was probably shorter than their labor pains; so, quite reasonably, I expected that my body would be able to do the same thing. I couldn't have been more wrong. In the first place, my body was 35-½ years old when I gave birth to my first child. Secondly, although I gained not even a quarter-of-an-inch in my ankles or thighs, my belly (by my eighth month) gained entrance to a room a good half-minute before I did. (My belly button beat it by ten seconds.) Thirdly, and I may be wrong about this, but I have this really funny feeling that Cher and those other women must have not only exercised, but undoubtedly cut back to less than 25,000 calories a day. That's the only thing I can possibly think of that could have resulted in their getting back to their pre-baby sizes while I, on the other hand, still had people asking me when my baby was due when she was five months old.

It's not like I didn't exercise at all. I could get that bentwood rocker going like crazy during those 2:00 A.M. feedings. Plus, I switched from peanut M&Ms to plain, left half of the whipped cream off my banana splits, the extra mozzarella off my pizzas, and cut back on the butterscotch topping on my sundaes. So, it's not like I wasn't even *trying* to lose weight or anything.

By the time Carly was ten months old, as a matter of fact, I had lost nearly three pounds. Then I found out I was pregnant with Chelsea.

So, there I was at 36 years of age — with two children younger than two years old — and I weighed more than I ever had. I was depressed. I was the "F" word (fat). I wasn't suicidal, but I was despondent. That was when I discovered that if one looked in the dictionary under "post-partum depression," one would find a picture of porky me.

It was at that point that I decided to do something about it — besides, of course, leaving some of the whipped cream off my banana splits. I resolved right then and there to invest in my first-ever workout video. Unfortunately, my first-ever exercise video was also the first one Jane Fonda ever made. I was new to this workout stuff; I just didn't know any better. What I really needed was a workout video made by someone like Shelley Winters or Captain Kangaroo. Jane Fonda is a mean, mean woman. She makes Leona Helmsley, Cruella DeVille, and Joan Crawford look like Mother Teresa. What a sadistic, angry person she must have been. "Go for the burn!" she commands. I'm thinking, "I'm going for a *Big Mac*, Jane. *You* go for the burn!"

I sold her video at a garage sale to a woman who made the mistake of ringing my doorbell at 6:00 A.M., even though the sale was advertised as starting at "8:00 A.M. — NO EARLYBIRDS, PLEASE." I sold it to her with the assurance (misconception?) that she'd absolutely love it. I didn't lie, however, when I told her there had been a tremendous difference in my weight (20 pounds, actually) between the day I bought the video and the day I sold it to her. What I didn't tell her was that the difference was a weight *gain*. Well, she shouldn't have awakened me two hours before the sale started!

After Jane failed miserably to lure me into the "Marvelous World of Working Out," I still realized that something had to be done before I sank farther into the "Miserable World of Muumuus, Caftans, and Tarps." That's when I learned that a prerequisite for becoming an aerobics instructor had to be permanent PMS. What else, besides raging hormones, could cause women to inflict that kind of pain on other women? "Faster, faster! Get those knees up, ladies! No pain, no gain!" Yeah, right. But my thinking is "No pain, no *pain*." It was then that I decided that taking a low-impact aerobics class was a mistake. It was also then that I started my unsuccessful search for a *no*-impact aerobics class. I was amazed to learn there *ain't* no such of a *thang*. Personally, I think there should be. I know for a fact that demand for such a class is very, very high.

That was when my husband suggested that I start going to the gym with him.

"Honey, what exactly is it that you *do* at the gym?" I asked him.

"I just work out," he responded, nonchalantly.

"Sweetie, it's not possible to *just* work out," I advised him. "One can *just* drop in. Or one can *just* run to the store to pick up a few things. One can even *just* eat one Lay's potato chip, if one tries really hard. But never, never, *never* does one *just* work out. That's like saying, 'Thanks, but I *just* can't eat another bite,' or a telemarketer saying 'I *just* need a minute of your time.' Besides, I've walked through the den when you've been watching those bulge-offs."

"Body-building competitions," he corrected, somewhat indignantly.

"Whatever," I said. "All I know is that I'd much rather be a little chunky than sacrifice my bosoms to the Nautilus god."

"What are you talking about?"

"Oh, I've seen the chests of those women in the bulge-offs. They look like washboards! Heck, Arnold Schwartzenegger has bigger boobs than they have! Upper lip hair is hereditary in my family. That's bad enough. Why would I want to work so hard for a 42-AAAA bra size?"

"I don't think you'd ever have to worry about that," he informed me. "Those women work out for hours every day, and have incredibly low-fat diets. They're extraordinarily disciplined. There's not even the remotest possibility that you'd ever look like they do."

Sensing this was somehow *not* a compliment, I inquired, "So, what you're saying is that I don't have the discipline it takes to get into shape. What you really mean is that in order to be *toned*, I must get to the point where I shave all visible hair from my body, slather myself with vegetable oil, tan myself to a Hole-in-the-Ozone Bronze, parade around in a thong bathing suit, and strain my muscles until I look like I don't have enough fiber in my diet — all in front of a bunch of strangers?"

"I never said that," he quickly responded. "All I meant was that you'll never be that firm."

"Excuse me?" I asked defensively.

"I meant to say *hard*. You'll never have to worry about being that hard."

"Is that what you think I should be — *hard*?"

"That's not what I'm saying at all. I'm just trying to reassure you that you'll never have to worry about losing your softness."

"So, now I'm flabby."

"'Soft' and 'flabby' aren't synonyms," he instructed. "You wouldn't refer to a down pillow as 'flabby,' would you? Or a baby's behind?"

"Of course not, but a down pillow and a baby's behind don't have an extra twenty pounds of fat stuffed in them, either."

"Well, the gym thing was just a suggestion," he said, wisely giving up.

I guess he meant well. It's just that I had been in the gym once before when his car was being repaired, and I had to pick him up; and I had no intention of ever grunting like that in a public place in front of strangers.

There had to be another option. But what? By this point, I had ruled out aerobics (too strenuous), jazzercise (too animated), bodybuilding (grunting and hard boobies), power-walking (looks stupid), biking (dogs), and even plain-ol' walking (the weather was always either too hot or too cold). All that stuff was too hard, too boring, or too embarrassing. Surely, there had to be some way I could get back into shape and enjoy doing it. What was it that I could do that was both fun and exercise all rolled into one? Dancing! I *love* to dance! It's great exercise, and it's fun! I had struck gold!

"So," I thought, "what are my dancing options?"

I knew Les probably wouldn't want to take me dancing four or five nights a week; consequently, I'd have to find an alternative.

"Dance class! That's it! I'll enroll in a tap-dancing class! It'll be fun, aerobic, and easy! Why didn't I think of this before?" I asked myself.

The very next day, I called Bunny Brinkerhoff's School of Dance, and got signed up for her next beginners' class, which, fortunately, started the following week. Bunny gave me a list of things I'd need for class, such as tap shoes, tights, a leotard, and a little sheer skirt.

I bought all those items, and showed up the following Saturday morning, as instructed. I was very excited. I was very excited, that is, until I saw the rest of Bunny's Beginners' Tap Class. The Ginger-Rogers-wannabe who was closest to me in age came nearly to my waist. I sold my tap shoes at my next garage sale.

There was no exercise stone I felt I had left unturned. That left me no choice but to die-t. I didn't want to. I love food. I'm not, as you may have been able to tell already, a very disciplined person. I'm not the kind of person who gets into denial of the little *somethings* that make me happy, e.g., banana pudding, fried chicken, pizza, candy, popcorn, Coca-Cola®, pecan pie, pancakes, biscuits and gravy, ... Well, you get the picture. I knew I couldn't do it by myself. I knew I needed help, but I was running out of hope and ideas when I just happened to be watching television and saw a commercial for one of those "diet supplement shakes" (you know the kind). So, I thought, "Hey! I love milkshakes. This just might work!" My self-confidence was renewed! Reinforcements were on the way! I was going to my class reunion in a size 6 dress!

Yeah, right.

I don't know what happened. I followed the directions — one nutritious (okay, maybe that part's true), delicious (if your taste buds have been burned off) shake in the morning, one for lunch, followed by a healthy dinner. HA! After just two eight-ounce milkshakes, some celery stalks, and a few carrot sticks all day long, honey, I went home and gnawed through the lock I'd installed on the refrigerator door.

That was when a friend, noting my despondency, suggested I purchase a personalized subliminal message weight-loss tape. She said she had lost 35 pounds within just three months after receiving hers. She was the first to admit she had no idea how it happened, or what the secret was behind the success of the tapes. All she knew was that they worked for her.

Was I excited! I got the 800 number from her and ordered my personalized tape that very day. For an extra $99.95, I had it delivered the following day. Time was of the essence.

That night, I put the tape into my tape player, put the earphones on, and was soon lulled to sleep by the peaceful sound of ocean waves lapping some sandy beach. I must admit to at least a little optimism. Unfortunately, that optimism proved to be very short-lived when I was awakened about an hour later by my baby's crying. That was when I discovered the "secret" of those subliminal messages cloaked in the hypnotic, rhythmic sounds of the ocean waves and the soft cries of the sea birds. Those had been replaced by the mesmerizing chant, "Rebel is a lardbutt. Rebel is a lardbutt. Rebel is a . . . ."

How *rude!*

TWINKIES® OR TREADMILLS

*S*o, *how's that new diet coming along*? my husband asked me last weekend.

"Mrmphrum crurmphclphl," I answered. It was the best I could do with the Twinkie® in my mouth.

"That well, huh?"

That was when I decided I'd better get back to the gym. Actually, "back to" makes it sound like I actually had an exercise regimen at one time. My family (including me) joined a gym last year. My husband and our two teenaged daughters work out faithfully. I worked out faithfully for nearly a week, sometime last year.

But when could I work out? Les and the girls go in the afternoons when all the machines have waiting lines. Not me. I won't even wait in line for *doughnuts*.

And the middle of the day? Nah. That's either too close to lunch or too soon after, which leaves no time at all except for early in the morning — *very* early in the morning.

The gym opens at 5:30 A.M.; so that's when I got there. I felt so proud of myself. Hopping out of bed, grabbing a can of Coke® on my way out the door; running back inside to change out of my pajamas; running out the door again. I was filled with pride in myself for finally doing the right thing. I *could* do this! Yes!

Then I got to the gym.

Very serious people, it seems, go to the gym at 5:30 A.M.-- people who look as if they never leave the gym. Men with necks even bigger than my thighs were there. Women who love to sweat were there. But worst of all, *she* was there. Right next to me. *Jogging* on the treadmill.

"Good morning!" she beamed at me.

"Good morning," I huffed and puffed. "Do you know how to turn this thing on?"

She had a ponytail — *blonde*, of course. She was one with her spandex. She was wearing a tiny cut-off top and below-the-knee pants, with one of those little thong thingies over them. They looked painful. And she had on makeup — not yesterday's, like I was wearing — real, just-put-on-this-morning makeup. Her workout clothes were all coordinated, and her shoes looked like they never saw life outside the gym.

I, conversely, had on my husband's eight-year-old Walk America hole-y and rusted T-shirt; his discarded swimming trunks (well, they're comfortable); tennis shoes covered with paint; and white athletic knee socks—one with no elastic at the top, so it was actually an anklet.

"I'm Bambi," Ms. Spandex said.

"Of course, you are," I thought.

Instead, I said — in gasps, "Hi, Bambi. I'm Rebel."

"*Rebel*? What a *cool* name! I think I'll name my *kids* Rebel!" she responded.

"*Ohhh*-kay," I thought.

"So, is this your first time here?" she asked.

I slowed down so that I could carry on a conversation. Actually, I could have tied my shoes and put together a jigsaw puzzle at the speed I was going.

"As a matter of fact, I joined last year, but stopped coming," I admitted.

"And you see what happens when you do that!" she scolded. "Or were you . . . like *this* before then, too?"

"Oh, yeah. I've been like *this* for quite some time."

"Well, don't worry too much about it. My grandma's like you, too."

"Your *grandma*? Don't you mean your *mother*?" I asked, hopefully.

"Oh, no, ma'am. That's my *mom* over there," she responded, pointing to yet another pony-tailed blonde, this one bicycling like the mean old woman in the tornado scene from "The Wizard of Oz."

"That's your *mother*?" I asked, not wanting to hear the answer.

"Yes, ma'am. She has just six percent body fat. Isn't that *unreal*? Even *I* have seven percent."

"I have seven percent body fat in my *left earlobe*," I said. "How does your mom manage that?"

"Well, she works out five days a week, doesn't eat bread, sugar or meat; takes tae kwon do, tap, kickboxing, and jazz classes; runs 17 miles a day; meditates; and teaches gymnastics and cheerleading. She used to be a cheerleader in high school," Slenderella informed me.

"Of course, she was," I said — once again, to myself.

"How long did it take her to get like that?" I asked.

"Oh, she's *always* been like that. She only gained 14 pounds when she was pregnant with me. And she lost all that the week after I was born. She's just never let herself go like most older women do. No offense."

"None taken," I lied. "Well, it's been nice chatting with you, Bamboo."

"Bambi," she corrected.

"Whatever. Have fun," I said as I shut down the treadmill.

I wonder if Krispy Kreme's "Hot Doughnuts Now" sign is on. I don't look good with a ponytail, anyway.

BABY DIAPERS

I've been cursed with a queasy stomach pretty much since birth. If I *saw* anyone throw up, I'd throw up; if I *heard* anyone throw up, I'd throw up. Heck, if I even heard anyone *talking about* throwing up, I'd throw up. Unbelievably, I didn't throw up when my biology class was required to dissect a frog. Fortunately, when I impaled the stinky, bloated, slimy, little green thing with my scalpel, I just passed out right then and there and gave myself a colossal concussion. Well, at least I didn't throw up.

As much as it shames me to admit this, in that respect (and many others), I haven't improved much with age. That point has been driven home time and time again since I've become a mother.

I was convinced that I had given birth to a tar baby the first time I changed my firstborn's diaper. And what a pleasant surprise *that was*. I guess this particular poopoo-substance subject matter was just overlooked by Dr. Spock, or maybe it was *Mr.* Spock, or whatever enlightened authority it was that I was trusting prenatally. All I knew was that I was not at all prepared for that disgusting little black blob that I discovered when I changed her first "at home" diaper. And something told me that whatever it was, it was certainly *not* what had made Jed Clampett a wealthy man. Nope, this was not "black gold, Texas tea" — and I was certainly not destined to live in the land of *see*-ment ponds as a result of this stuff in my baby's diaper.

My maternal instincts, while basically untried, were even stronger than my well-conditioned gag reflex. Consequently, nausea quickly gave way to hysteria.

"*Les!*" I screamed to my husband, "Come and *look* at this! There's something terribly wrong with the baby!"

He tore down the hall, leaving skid marks on the floor as he screeched to a halt at the baby's changing table.

"*Gross!*" he shrieked, covering his mouth and nose with his hand. "What *is* that?"

"How would *I* know?" I babbled. "Just finish changing her,

please. I'm going to call her pediatrician to find out just what process it is that breaks breast milk down into hardened axle grease."

"Wait!" he implored. "What am I supposed to use to *clean* this?"

"Try the wipies," I suggested, on my way out of the nursery. "If those don't work, yell, and I'll bring the putty knife!"

When I returned, the baby was crying, and poor Les looked as if he were on the verge of tears, as well.

He informed me, rather pitifully, "She just laid another two pounds of *asphalt*! It took me 18 minutes and 67 wipies to get her clean; and as soon as I did, she just turned around and dropped another load — and then, . . . and then . . . she *smiled* at me when she finished! I think we got the wrong baby, you know? I think this one's *possessed* or something. This just can't be . . . *normal*, can it?"

"Honey, she's not possessed. She's just a baby," I reassured him. "But at least I did find out that she's not an alien. Dr. Brown said the black blobs *are* normal, and that they're certainly not anything we should worry about. She also said the baby would stop doing this in the next day or so."

"Great," he responded, smiling with relief. "But did she happen to mention what *color* the next batch is gonna be?"

"Nope, but I'm sure it'll be normal."

Boy, was I wrong.

Without going into unnecessary detail, suffice it to say that it was a year before I could eat mustard on a hot dog again.

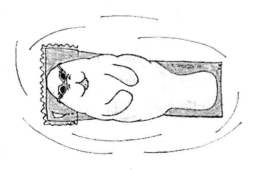

THE DINNER PARTY

T here was an article in the newspaper recently with tips to help a hostess prepare for a "fabulous dinner party." I have to admit the advice given was certainly sound. As a matter of fact, if followed, those tips couldn't help but lead to a dinner party so successful that it would be talked about for years. But, heck, mine are talked about for years without my having to go to all that trouble.

The "experts" suggest, among other things, that as much as *two to four weeks* ahead, one get out the invitations, and rent the chairs, tables, dishes, glasses, flatware, and whatever else one might need.

At our house, four weeks is too far ahead to even plan for *Christmas*, much less a dinner party.

The real *two-weeks-ahead* scenario at our house would be:

Me: "Honey, let's have a dinner party."

Him: "Let's not."

Me: "So, who do you want to invite?"

Him: "Nobody."

Me: "Okay. I'll get on the phone tomorrow and invite everybody."

Him: "I'm not coming."

The experts tell us that *one to two weeks* ahead, we should plan what we're going to serve, including when to start preparing it; and they advise us that we should be sure that we have all the proper serving pieces.

Here's the conversation at our house one week before:

Me: "I guess I should start calling people about the dinner party."

Him: "What dinner party?"

With only *three to five days* left, the specialists suggest you make sure your table coverings are cleaned and pressed. They also recommend that you be sure the outfit you're going to wear is ready. Oh, yes — pick up those rental items, and make sure your shopping list is complete.

Our house (three to five days left):

Me: "I really should make those calls."

Him: "I'm not coming."

*Three da*ys ahead, they tell us to clean the house and our serving pieces, and to prepare whatever needs to be done ahead, food-wise.

Our house:

Me: "I really should . . . ."

Him: "I'm not . . . ."

And, with just a couple of days left before the gala, the experts recommend we set up the bar, select the music, set the table, put out the serving dishes, and, of course, arrange the decorations. With just one day left, we should finish our make-ahead recipes; buy ice, flowers, and other stuff that won't last long; and take a final look at our house. (A "final" look? Are we moving?)

At our house:

Me: "Hi, Kath. It's Rebel. I know it's late notice, but do you and Mike have plans for tomorrow night?"

Him: "Tell her to tell Mike I won't be here."

On the day of the party, "they" tell us to "post a list of foods so you don't forget anything" and "allow at least one hour to catch your breath, relax and get ready." How funny.

D-Day (or P-Day):

1:00 P.M.: I'm at the grocery store. My cart is loaded down with appetizers (pretzels), entrée (bottled spaghetti sauce, prepackaged salads, frozen garlic bread), and dessert (ice cream sandwiches).

2:00 P.M.: I'm at home, cleaning by throwing all non-perishables into closets and drawers; yelling to the kids to find the vinyl tablecloth and scrape the dried food off it; and sending Les to borrow the neighbors' card tables and folding chairs (or lawn chairs or porch swings or whatever they have to spare), all the while admonishing him to cross his fingers when he tells the *non*-invitees that we're just having a "family reunion."

4:00 P.M.: I'm tearing clothes out of my closet, trying them on, throwing them on the floor, stomping on them, and vowing to get back to the gym tomorrow if just *one thing* fits. I finally find a lime-green and hot-pink polyester muumuu my Aunt Mae left at our house last summer.

5:00 P.M.: I call Janet (a non-invitee) to borrow her large platter. She informs me that I never returned it after my Labor Day "family reunion."

5:45 P.M.: I jump into the shower and remember that I was supposed to buy shampoo and conditioner at the store. I wash my hair with mildew remover and condition it with shaving cream.

6:00 P.M. (When the guests are supposed to start arriving): My magnifying mirror lies shattered on the floor; consequently, it looks like Tammy Faye Bakker has applied my makeup. My hair won't dry (I guess it's the shaving cream). I look like Hitler in drag at a luau.

6:10 P.M.: Thank goodness, no one has arrived yet. I'm appalled to hear the drone of rap music coming from the stereo. (I had asked my teenaged daughters to put on some *music*.) I warn them that they have exactly 10 seconds to replace it with *real* music, or be confined to quarters until they're old enough to be greeters at Wal-Mart. They do it in *four* seconds.

6:15 P.M.: The doorbell rings.

They're H-E-E-E-E-R-E!

The garlic bread is still frozen. The ice cream sandwiches aren't.

THE FIVE WORDS
MEN FEAR MOST

H aving been married all these years to a man who can make a mime seem like Joan Rivers, it still amazes me to see the reaction in his eyes and the sheer terror on his face when I speak those five most frightful (to men) words: "Honey, we need to talk."

His face turns flour-white, his eyes get all beady and totally glaze over, his bottom lip quivers like a Chihuahua and, for just a split second, he actually seems to whimper.

"*Why*?" he beseeches, shuddering. "Didn't we already talk this month? What did I *do*?"

"You didn't *do* anything, sweetie," I reassure him. "There's just something I need to talk to you about."

"But I don't *want* to talk."

"Honey, this won't take long. I promise."

"Was this the 'worse' in that 'for better or for worse' part of our wedding vows?"

"You're really making too much of this, you know."

"Or is this what they mean in that 'til death do you part' part?" he asks.

"Don't you think you're being a little overly dramatic?" I ask. "You don't even know what I want to talk to you about."

"No, but I *do* know that I'm not going to be happy when we're finished."

"Why in the world are you so paranoid? It's just a little discussion I'm seeking — not *blood*."

"I'd rather give blood. It's not nearly as scary. I'd rather spend an entire night with Dracula — at his place in Transylvania, with nary a cross nor a garlic necklace to my name. I really, *really* don't want to do this. *Please* don't make me talk," he entreats.

"Now you're being ridiculous."

"I am *not*," he attempts to assure me. "Isn't there *anything* else I can do? I'll clean out the refrigerator. I'll do the laundry and cook for the next six months. I'll even take the girls to the mall anytime they want to go. Just *please* don't make me do this!"

"What harm will it do you just to talk to me about something really important?"

"I'll throw up. I *know* I'll throw up. I'm already feeling a little queasy. I'm telling you I can't *do* this. If you *really* loved me, you wouldn't even ask me. Why don't you just write me — or, better yet, *E-mail* me. Okay? That would work! Yeah! That would be perfect! And then I could answer you by computer. Wouldn't that be good? That would be really good. And I wouldn't have to barf."

"What is *wrong* with you? You are being totally psychotic about this. You don't even have the slightest idea what I want to talk to you about, yet you're going berserk."

"You know how coyotes and wolves and other animals will actually gnaw their own foot off to escape a trap? Well, this is a lot like that. It's just as bad — only it's my *whole body*, and I can't chew enough of me off to get out of this one. It's like a really bad dream. *Please* don't make me talk! I *hate* this!"

"I've never heard anything so ridiculous in my entire life, you know. But if you're that adamant about this, I guess there's nothing I can do about it. I'm not going to *make* you talk."

"You're *not*?" he asks as his color returns, his eyes unglaze, and his bottom lip firms up.

"No. If you feel that strongly about not wanting to talk, then I'm certainly not going to force you."

"Oh, thanks, honey. Thanks for understanding. I really appreciate that. It's just that . . . well, you know how I hate to talk," he attempts to rationalize.

"Yes, I know very well how you hate it," I say, as I reluctantly give up on trying to communicate with Mute Man.

As he walks off, the phone rings. He picks it up.

"Hello," he says. "Hey, man! What's up? No kidding? That sounds great! Sure, I can make that. It'll be like old times. Great! See you then!"

He hangs up the phone and turns to me.

"That was Brian. A bunch of us guys are getting together Saturday. We're gonna charter a boat and go deep-sea fishing. Man, that'll be so much fun! Just sittin' around, chewin' the fat, and catchin' up on old times!"

Maybe I should quit saying, "Honey, we need to talk." I think perhaps, "Honey, let's chew some . . . *fat*" would be *far* less intimidating. *I'd* be the one to throw up, but what the heck? At least, we'd be talking.

THE EVOLUTION OF UNDERWEAR THROUGHOUT MARRIAGE

I can, after more than 20 years of marriage, only vaguely recall what my "wedding night" negligee looked like. I'm fairly certain, however, that words such as "alluring" and "seductive" are pretty appropriate descriptions. I can also just faintly remember, in the first years of our marriage, bikini panties, those wonderful French push-you-up, push-you-out, push-you-together bras, and the sensuous little teddies. Unfortunately, the teddies have been replaced by (if I must assign a name to them) what would have to be called *floyds*. And those delicate, sexy, uplifting French "enhancers" have been supplanted (at least for me) by industrial-strength bras, i.e., the sort that are worn by 5'10", 375-pound, mustachioed Russian women with names like "Nikita" or "Boris."

And those bikini panties, which would have do some serious stretching to fit even a Barbie® doll, can no longer be found in my dresser drawer. What one *will* find, however, are good, sensible cotton briefs that look so much like my husband's I have to check them *very* closely before I separate "his" from "hers" on Laundry Day.

And, of course, the garter belts and thigh-high stockings are only a distant memory. They're much too impractical; besides thigh-high stockings would, beyond any doubt, result in immediate gangrene, what with the instantaneous and complete lack of blood flow to any areas below my thighs. So, what I have now are your basic control-top, reinforced support hose, unconditionally guaranteed to hide varicose veins the size of the Snake River.

The flimsy peignoir has been replaced by an extra-large University of Alabama T-shirt in the spring and summer, and a sweatsuit and white athletic socks in the fall and winter. And, because I realize that variety *is* the spice of life, I have been known to don long-sleeved, turtleneck, flannel pajamas (complete with the rear drop-flap and the aforementioned athletic socks) in extremely cold weather. One can only imagine the difficulty my husband has in restraining himself on those particular nights. Poor baby. I'm such a *tease*.

He just can't bring himself to completely give up on re-supplying my lingerie drawers. Just last year, for Valentine's Day, the poor, hopeful darling bought me a silk camisole with matching tap pants. I discovered that night that tap pants give me a wedgie.

I don't know what happens to sexy lingerie — or sexy underwear for men — between the honeymoon and the kids. Maybe it has something to do with stretch marks, love handles, varicose veins, beer bellies, and thunder thighs. Who knows? And it's certainly not that I wouldn't enjoy the sensual luxury of all those Pandora's Secret dainties. It's just that I prefer to enjoy them in the privacy of my own dresser drawers. I'm not about to wear them in front of my husband. He's just "this" side of that phenomenon known as *mid-life crisis*. Why give him reason to run into the arms of a 20-year-old, like my friend Angie Womack's husband did? At least, that (the mid-life crisis) was her husband's excuse. On their Divorce Petition, where it usually lists something like "Irreconcilable Differences" or "Adultery," he had his lawyer insert "Wife wears *extremely* unattractive underwear and nightclothes."

When the judge asked Angie's husband's lawyer to be more specific, he said, "Well, Your Honor, Mr. Womack has stated, in no uncertain terms, that his wife wears granny grunts and industrial-strength cotton bras under her clothes, *and* she wears *flannel* nightgowns and athletic socks — to *bed*!"

"DIVORCE GRANTED!" bellowed the pale and trembling judge, as his gavel hit its target.

Maybe I should give the tap pants just one more try.

OH, HONEY, YOU'RE NOT REALLY GOING TO WEAR *THAT*, ARE YOU?

O ne can simply *look* at some men to be able to conclude instantly that they're unmarried. This particular marital status cannot be determined necessarily by their joyful demeanor, the perpetual smile on their faces, or even that exaggerated little lilt in their step. It's as simple as looking at the clothes they're wearing.

Recently, I saw a man being interviewed on CNN. Poor soul, he was wearing a grayish-green tweed coat, a burgundy and blue striped shirt, and (heaven forbid) a pink and neon green plaid tie. I knew right away that he had no wife. No self-respecting woman would allow her husband to even go out of the house dressed like that, let alone be on national television.

Granted, this *is* a new millennium; consequently, the woman helping a man avoid public ridicule might not necessarily be his wife. However, there are certain responsibilities that accompany wedding vows — unspoken perhaps, but responsibilities just the same. One of the most significant of these is the usually soundless covenant a wife makes to her husband on their wedding day that she will do everything — as God is her witness — *everything* in her power to prevent her husband from shaming himself (and *her*self, in particular) by wearing clothes *he* feels should be worn together. That pitiful CNN interview*ee* is only one example. There are so few men capable of actually going into their closets and chests-of-drawers and selecting an "ensemble." "Costume" would be a better description of what they customarily pick. And the more pieces the outfit contains, the higher the likelihood of humiliation. They can generally do pretty well with sweatshirts, T-shirts, gym shorts — outfits that don't really count.

It frightens me nearly to death when my husband goes out of town overnight, or longer, on business. To him, anything not white, blue, brown, green, black or yellow is *red*. Burgundy is red, orange is red, rust is red, fuchsia is red, pink is red. Well, you get the general idea.

The poor baby once nearly left the house wearing a royal blue sport shirt with navy slacks. To him, you see, "blue is blue." This is a man who, miraculously, knows not to wear black shoes with a brown suit or brown shoes with a gray or black suit. Beyond that, he knows absolutely no hue distinction.

And, while I certainly don't want to come across as sexist, fact is, this color-blindness is primarily a *man* thing. Granted, an infinitesimal number of women *do* suffer from this affliction; but most of us have sense enough not to leave the house in a lime green tank top and pine green stirrup pants. Actually, most of us have sense enough not to even leave our *closets* wearing tank tops or stirrup pants of *any* color.

The vast majority of married or "involved" men I know pretty much owe the way they dress to the woman they're married to or involved with. For instance, according to his wife, my husband's co-worker Mike Barker showed up for their (his and Melissa's, not his and my husband's) first date in a chartreuse leisure suit, purple-and-hot-pink polyester shirt, white belt, and red patent-leather platform shoes — and that was in *1997*. His date (and soon-to-be wife), Melissa, saw the diamond-in-the-rough that was Mike, took pity on him, and made it her mission in life to rehabilitate this poor man. And she's done a wonderful job. Mike's only lapse was when Melissa had to go out of town to take care of a sick relative, and Mike ran out of pre-matched (by Melissa) outfits. (Her one-week stay was unexpectedly extended).

I was on the phone on the eighth day of Melissa's trip when I got an emergency break-in call from a secretary in my husband's office. It seems that Mike had shown up for work in a blue coat, orange and pink madras shirt, kelly green slacks and a red, white and yellow striped tie — and *wing tips* — with *white* socks. It was clear to all the women in the office that this poor man was suffering from "wife withdrawal."

"Please send him home immediately," I urged the secretary. "Tell him I'll meet him there!"

"Ten-four!" she responded. I could hear her shouting, "Get him out of the building and home — STAT!"

Incredibly, Mike arrived at his house at exactly the same time I did. Some might call it fate.

"*Rebel*! Thank *heaven* you're here! Please help me!" the poor thing pleaded. "I really thought I looked fine when I left home. Then I saw how all the women in the office looked at me! The pity in their eyes! It was terrible. I felt like such a *freak*! Melissa wasn't supposed to be gone this long! What will I do? How can I go on dressing without her?"

"Poor baby," I soothed as best I could. Although I was still a bit shaky, I knew that Mike really needed for me to be strong. "Don't worry. I'm here now. Quick — take me to your closet!"

It was less than five minutes later that the phone rang. Mike was busy changing out of his amazing technicolor costume, so I answered it.

"Hello," I said, much more composed now. "Barker residence."

"Rebel? Rebel, is that *you*?" (It was a frantic Melissa.)

"Yes, Melissa. It's me — and everything's okay. *Really.* There's no reason for you to worry."

"Thank *heaven* you're there! Oh, if I'd only known I'd be gone so long, I could have laid out enough clothes to see him through! What kind of wife *am* I?"

"Don't be so hard on yourself," I consoled. "Sometimes we just can't see these things coming. You had no way of knowing. It happens to all of us sooner or later. There's absolutely nothing you could have done to prevent it." I reminded her of the time my husband, Les, had gone on a business trip to Chicago, supposedly for only three days. I begged him to take a couple of extra pre-orchestrated outfits "just in case." But *no*! "Real men" don't even take "outfits" — much less "extra" outfits.

"If I run out of the pre-orchestrated stuff, there's a laundry service in the hotel. Believe me, I'll manage just fine," he insisted.

Needless to say, his group got snowed in. That was when they decided that as long as they were there, they may as well go ahead and have pictures taken for the front page of the company's *national* newsletter. My only consolation is that my husband obviously wasn't the only one whose wife packed just enough coordinated outfits for the number of days the session was supposed to have lasted. Consequently, the (unfortunately) *color* photograph that made it into the newsletter was composed of some of the most revolting, offensive, vile fashion mistakes ever to make the printed page. There on the right side of the front row was the director of the seminar dressed in a wine and navy striped dress shirt, and red, yellow, and light blue plaid slacks. Beside him and in the three rows above were the sales agents, looking as if this were Clown College Graduation Day. There was one man dressed in a yellow-and-green-plaid shirt with red-and-blue-plaid slacks (the thinking there is "Plaid is plaid, right?"); one was dressed in a hot-pink pullover, kelly-green blazer and yellow, double-knit slacks (his wife still, to this day, swears she has absolutely no idea how those even got into his garment bag); and there, in the very center of the front row, was Les — in his gym shorts, Beatles T-shirt, flip-flops and paisley tie.

And I was worried.

FOOD IS NOT JUST FOR EATING

It's both my personal opinion and experience that any woman who marries a man whose mother is a wonderful cook is a masochist (to the third power), unless, of course, she (the wife) is also an excellent cook. I am a masochist.

I've never denied either my ability to blacken *any* food I cook, or my sorrow at the demise in popularity of this particular cuisine. Fortunately, my expertise in cooking extends far beyond that one culinary skill. For instance, I have created giblet gravy that has also proven to be a perfectly suitable substitute for my children's school glue. I simply remove the giblets and add a little extra flour. My husband caulked two bathtubs with my pancake batter. My dill weed dip is now holding the soap dish to the wall in our guest bath. (That dill smell disappears completely within a week or two). My resourceful husband has also discovered that my french fries make excellent kindling — particularly if I use extra-long potatoes.

It was one of the high points of my life when one of the teenage boys in our neighborhood came to my door, explaining that he had heard about my blackened skillet cornbread. He asked if I would mind making *twenty* of them for him. He even offered to pay me for my time and ingredients. Of course, I was so overwhelmed and flattered that someone not only appreciated, but *sought*, my cooking, I told him I wouldn't *dream* of taking any money from him; just the fact that he had asked was payment enough. My giddiness bubble burst a few weeks later, however, when I drove by his house and saw his car, minus its front tires, propped up on my skillet cornbread — ten under each front wheel.

And then there were my blackened biscuits, which my Great-Uncle Vondy proclaimed, "could kill a bull yearling at a hundred yards." These gastronomical disasters debuted during the first and, as the result of popular demand, *last* of the big family Christmas brunches my husband and I hosted a few years ago. In order to maintain the tradition established years before by my mother-in-law, I knew I had no choice but to make "scratch" biscuits, i.e., biscuits made from certain dry ingredients, short'nin', eggs, and buttermilk. Given my track record in the kitchen, this was an undertaking of gargantuan scale. You see, my experience with cooking biscuits prior to that Christmas had consisted of peeling the shiny, paper covering from the can and pressing a spoon against the seam, which action was followed immediately by a loud, popping sound as the dough burst from the can. Personally, I viewed this as no small task.

Contributing greatly to my anxiety was the fact that my mother-in-law's biscuits were always devoured with such accompanying comments as, "I *declare*, Silverin (the aforementioned biscuit-cooker), you'd better get some of Emery's (the biscuit-cooker's husband) fishing sinkers to tie these biscuits down before we have to climb a ladder to get them off the ceiling!"; and "Silverin, I realize I'm holding one of your biscuits, but if I wasn't looking at it with my own eyes, I'd *swear* it was a feather!"; and "Shoot, I've held *marshmallows* heavier than these biscuits!" So you see what I was up against.

Nonetheless, I found what promised to be a "fail-proof" recipe, and psyched myself to the point that I felt that I could really pull this off. I even visualized the rush to fill my ultra-weightless gourmet's delights with butter, ham, cheese and sweet, pickled bell peppers, as our guests, my husband, kids, and I had all done for so many Christmases at my in-laws'. I even made *eight dozen* biscuits in anticipation of the rush for them that my mother-in-law had experienced for hers year after year.

Imagine my *surprise* when everyone, not even halfway through their first biscuit, suddenly remembered — and *revealed* — their holiday weight-loss regimens, all of which called for the total exclusion of bread from their diets. It seemed, however, that they *were* allowed all the ham (store-bought, coincidentally), cheese (also store-bought), and pickled bell peppers (prepared by [who else?] my mother-in-law) they could eat.

Strange diet, but who am I to question anyone's personal nutritional preferences? And although I was disappointed that my biscuits were to be sacrificial lambs to the Diet God, I tried to understand.

What was even more puzzling, however, was my husband's startled (and I felt "over-") reaction when he later discovered me tossing the uneaten biscuits out to the birds and squirrels.

"What are you *doing*?" he screamed in horror.

"Well," I replied, "I didn't want all these biscuits to go completely to waste."

Then I could've *sworn* I heard him mumble something under his breath about those poor birds not ever being able to get off the ground again.

"What did you say?" I asked him.

"Well, I was just thinking aloud that they're probably not very nutritionally sound food for birds and squirrels. Why don't we just wrap them in foil and box them up? I have a much better use for them," he suggested.

And I thought, "Bless his sweet heart. I'll bet he's going to take them to the homeless shelter. Those folks would really appreciate my biscuits."

Silly, naïve me. The truth came a short time later in the form of an Overnight Express envelope from a National Hockey League team. Inside the envelope was a $50.00 check, accompanied by an order for another two dozen "homemade hockey pucks."

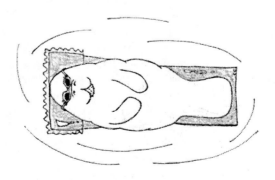

"MOM! WHAT'S FOR DINNER?"

Those words have been known to strike fear in even the most stouthearted of moms, of which I am not one. I've cooked boneless rumps and rumpless bones, and livers and gizzards, and givers and lizzards, and noodles and strudels, and taters and beans the same way over and over hundreds of times more than I care to remember. It would probably stun many of my good friends to learn how little imagination I have when it comes to chicken and ground beef, the creative playgrounds of cooks the world over. As hard as it is for me to admit, I'm afraid there's not a creative culinary bone in my entire body.

After having cooked what has to be thousands of meals, I've reached the point of being just totally brain dead when it comes to cooking. I just can't seem to get very excited about experimenting with new recipes. Besides, mine never turn out to look or taste anything at all like the ones in the books. Like the time, last week, when I made Beef Wellington. I was particularly pleased with myself because this meal did at least *look* like the illustration in the book — if you just looked at the food, and didn't look for the china, crystal, silver, place cards, Irish linen tablecloth and napkins, and centerpiece in the illustration. Unfortunately, my pleased-with-myself bubble burst when my husband took his first bite.

"I thought you were going to cook Beef Wellington tonight," he said, swallowing with great difficulty.

"This *is* Beef Wellington," I responded, defensively.

"Oh," he replied.

"And just what does *that* mean?" I asked in my most offended tone.

"Nothing. I guess this is just a different recipe than what we had at Chez Pierre," he answered, beads of sweat rapidly forming on his upper lip, while his eyes darted about the room in frantic search of an escape route.

"Well, of course, it's different! *Their* chef learned to cook at the Cordon Bleu — *yours* flunked Home Ec! But that's not what you meant. I think you were suggesting that this tastes nothing at all like Beef Wellington, weren't you?"

"Of course not," he replied as great rivulets of sweat poured from his face. "I mean, I can see meat and stuff in there and all, and I can taste some spices. It's just *different*. That's all."

"'Different' how?" I interrogated relentlessly.

"*Good* different," the doomed, trapped thing responded. I could tell by the rate at which his nose was growing that he wasn't telling me the truth; but since he was telling me what I wanted to hear, I took mercy on him.

"Thank you, darling," I cooed. "Tomorrow night, I'm fixing Lobster Thermidor."

"Can't wait," he mumbled, as his nose knocked over his iced tea glass.

IF I PROMISE NOT TO COOK,
WILL YOU COME FOR DINNER?

I 'm running out of people to invite to our house for dinner
parties, cookouts, brunches — whatever occasion it is that
would bring people over to eat. Most of our friends have already
eaten with us; and those who haven't have talked to those who
have. Perhaps if I promised that Les would cook, ...

I come from a family of good cooks. What happened to me?
Isn't there a "cooking gene?" If I have to inherit upper lip hair and
a huge rear end, isn't it only fair that I should also be able to cook
at least half as well as the rest of my extended family?

I don't know what happens to me in the kitchen. I follow the
recipe directions explicitly. That doesn't seem to matter. My
pumpkin pies look like seismologists' miniature replicas of the
San Andreas Fault. My cakes look like Mount St. Helens -- after
the eruption. My fried chicken crust *slinks* off like skin shed by a
snake.

When my youngest daughter was four, she asked me one night
at dinner (home-cooked) why we were all having to share just one
pancake. She also asked where the syrup was. The "pancake" she
referred to was actually my version of skillet cornbread. I guess
the people who wrote the cookbook were pretty serious about that
self-rising cornmeal.

And then there was the time I prepared that good ol' Southern
favorite, chicken and dumpling. No, that's not a typo. It was
really just *a* dumpling — *one* dumpling. I have no idea where I
went wrong. I mixed everything from scratch. I rolled out the
dough stuff. I flattened it with the roller. And I even sliced them
up into four separate and distinct . . . *things.* Then I dumped them
into the pan with the chicken, which was mostly stuck to the
bottom after the water sort of cooked out. It all cooked for an
hour . . . or two . . . or maybe three. I can't remember. I was
watching "Gone With the Wind," so I guess I wasn't paying all
that much attention. All I know is that I put the dumplings in
when the teenaged Scarlett was deciding which of her wanna-be
beaus was going to be lucky enough to go and fetch her dessert at
the barbecue at Twelve Oaks; and I took them off the burner when
Rhett gave her the "Frankly, my dear" dressing-down before he
left for Charleston. So, I guess it was a pretty good while that they
cooked.

"What is *this*?" my 11-year-old, Chelsea, asked as she sat down at the dinner table.

"Good grief! I think I just gave myself a hernia lifting this bowl!" exclaimed my husband, dropping the dish onto the table, which shook and sagged. "How much flour did you use in this?"

"A bag," I replied.

"A *bag*? A *bag*? What *size* bag?" he asked, holding his side.

"I don't know. Just a bag — maybe ten pounds."

"Ten pounds of flour would feed the Waltons *and* the Bradys!" he declared. "Why is it in a . . . *lump* like that?"

"Don't ask me. I just dropped the four thingies in there and they just sort of fused into one."

"What do you mean when you say '*thingies*'?" he asked, warily.

"Oh, you know. The little dumpling thingies."

"There should be about fifty little dumpling *thingies* — not *four*," he informed me.

"Well, excuse me, *Julia Child*! The recipe didn't say how many dumplings to make. I just sort of guessed. There are four of us, so I just assumed four dumplings would be plenty."

"Except that instead of *four* dumplings, we're eating one *colossal* dumpling," said Carly, my 13-year-old. "It looks like something the kids cooked on 'The Little Rascals.' It's probably going to *blow up* when we cut into it."

"Can we even *cut* into it?" asked her little sister.

"I don't think we have a knife with a blade strong enough. Maybe the chainsaw will do the trick," added their dad, prompting an outburst of spontaneous laughter.

"Very funny," I said.

Instead of the chainsaw, we stuck metal shish-ka-bob skewers into the dumpling and all lifted it out together. That way no one got hurt. The chicken clung to the sides of the dumpling like those little suckerfish on sharks.

After trying unsuccessfully to actually cut into the offending mass, we wisely gave up, and went out for Chinese.

When we returned home, we found Chili, our Chihuahua, sprawled on the sofa; "evidence" smeared across her little black face. She had made her way onto the table and helped herself. Half the gob was gone. Poor baby. She didn't look very good. Carly and Chelsea lifted her (it took both of them) and gently placed her in her bed. She had rug burns for several days — on her belly.

SHE'S THE BEST *WHAT*
IN MOBILE COUNTY?

M y precious, little maternal grandmother characterized, to me, the "sweet Southern grandmother" in the truest sense. "Mamaw" was warm, loving, giving, and probably the best cook in Mobile, if not the entire state of Alabama.

Her energy was inexhaustible. She had a one-acre vegetable garden that she tilled, tended, and harvested in the steamy Alabama summers well into her seventies. And no amount of pleading or scolding could persuade her of the hardship she was placing on her aging little body. Warnings of possible heat stroke or other hazards to her health only made her that much more determined to show all of us that she was "up to the task."

She drove this point home vigorously, as a matter of fact, at one of our large family reunions many years ago. The hope, among all her children, was that, perhaps together, they could persuade her to give up her beloved, yet perilous, garden. They gently bombarded her with a long list of things that she, at her advanced age, should not be doing – not the least of which was hoeing. In order to spare Mamaw any embarrassment, this conversation was held (they thought) out of the range of hearing of the more than one hundred other relatives attending. I can only imagine the shock of those hundred plus when they heard this feisty, diminutive, God-fearing matriarch yell (very loudly, I might add) at her grown children, in rage, frustration, indignation, and self-defense, "I'll have every single one of you know that even at 76 years of age, I am *still* the best HOER in Mobile County!"

TUBBERWARE

I spent the night at my mom's not long ago, after having returned too late and too tired from an arts and crafts shopping marathon with her in Mississippi to attempt to drive the 50 miles to my house.

Mom was still asleep when I awoke; and since I have to have "a little something" to eat first thing every morning, I put a couple of slices of bread in the toaster. I'd love to be able to say that, at that point, I ate the dry toast with a cup of black, decaffeinated coffee. I'd love to, but I can't. So, after creaming and sugaring my high-octane New Orleans chicory, I returned to the refrigerator in search of margarine. I was delighted to find that I had my choice of butter, oleo, margarine, or "spread," whatever in the world *that* is. I opted for butter. Imagine my surprise when I opened the container and found . . . *turnip greens*. Fortunately, Mom had yet another butter tub in the fridge. Surprise again — *mashed potatoes*.

"Oh, well. I must be getting closer. I know for a fact that Mom puts butter in her mashed potatoes," I said to myself as I opened a third container -- this time, a margarine tub. "This has *got* to be margarine. What *is* this? It looks like . . . . Oh, *gross!* Boiled rutabagas!"

The fourth opening — that of the "oleo" — was no more successful than the others. As a matter of fact, it was worse. It rendered something that looked vaguely like leftover anchovy pound cake.

By that time, I was pretty terrified at the prospect of opening what was labeled "Spread with Sweet Cream," even though it *promised* — right there on the lid — "25% less fat than butter or margarine," neither of which seemed to occupy any space in my mom's refrigerator, anyway. Surely, I hoped, surely, *this* — the last of the butter/oleo/margarine/spread tubs — will contain something yellow. Well, it did — sardines packed in mustard.

I discovered that day that my mom has an entire set of *Tubber*ware. There must have been 75 of the recycled containers in her cabinets. Combined with those in her fridge, that gave her a total of more than 100.

That was also the day I learned that cold mashed potatoes on toast isn't really all that bad, if you're hungry — really, really hungry. Or, as Fabio says, "I cahn't be-LEEF id's nod BAH-da!"

Believe it, Hair Boy, it's *not* butter!

HYMNS ARE GREAT FOR DROWNING OUT REPRIMANDS

M y little maternal grandmother, "Mamaw," daughter of a Southern Baptist preacher, and loyal member of Shadowlawn Baptist Church well into her 90s, reluctantly resigned, at age 88, to give up her independence and move in with my mom, the eldest of her seven children, and, like Mamaw, a widow.

At the time Mamaw moved in with my mother, Mom was 70 years old herself; so here we have a granny taking care of a granny — a scary enough pairing. Not only that, but we were all about to learn that patience was not Mom's strong suit. As if that weren't bad enough, she (my mom) is just one massive, ambulatory, exposed nerve. She's the only person I've ever known who can shred a beverage napkin into over 17,000,000 pieces during just one baby shower. She's what could very appropriately be described as a "nervous shredder." This is a woman who could put Freddy Kruger to shame. If the producers of "Nightmare on Elm Street" and all its sequels ever decide to kill Freddy off for good and revive the film series using his long-lost momma, Heddy Kruger, I've got their female lead all ready for them.

If there's no napkin nearby, she'll shred whatever's handy — the paper that straws come in at fast food restaurants, newspapers, currency — it doesn't matter, as long as it's shreddable. She doesn't do it consciously; it's just her own form of Valium®, I suppose.

And, of course, having Mamaw in the house 24/7 got her nerves in even more of an uproar. There couldn't have been two more strong-willed, mule-headed women on the face of God's green earth; and here they were — at 88 and 70 years of age — sharing a home, which is something neither of them had done for a very long time, with anyone.

Enter disaster.

Mom, realizing the only alternative to Mamaw's living with her was to put her into a nursing home, was bound and determined to make this less-than-ideal situation work — no matter what.

As so often happens when children reach retirement age or older (or sometimes younger), the parent/child relationship throws itself, with wild abandon, into reverse. Mom's and Mamaw's was no different. Mamaw was constantly testing the waters of her new frontier (Mom's home, hence, domain), and was quite disinclined to renounce her independence, even though her hearing, eyesight, memory, and judgment were rapidly failing.

Her efforts to retain her independence manifested themselves in many ways, not the least of which was cooking. But while Mamaw could recount, even to the most minute detail, her first date with my late grandfather, she would forget having put on a pot of water to boil for grits. As a result, Mom lived in constant fear of having her home burned to the ground — with her mother in it.

Mamaw also insisted on growing a little vegetable garden in the backyard. While that, in and of itself, did not constitute a real danger to Mamaw, her going up and down back porch stairs she couldn't even see did pose actual jeopardy to her frail little bones.

And then there was her determination to keep track of her daily medication, in all its vast and sundry forms, all by herself.

Because of all this — and more, poor Mom, cocktail napkin (and sometimes *cocktail*) in hand, would have to keep Mamaw under constant surveillance. This vigil annoyed and insulted Mamaw to no end, and she rebelled against it in her own inimitable fashion — she *sang*.

The seriousness of the violation that resulted in Mom's reprimand determined the particular hymn with which Mamaw would counter. For instance, if Mom had to scold Mamaw for once again attempting to take her medication without Mom's supervision, Mamaw would anchor her hands over her ears, scrunch her eyes closed, and launch into "Amazing Grace." If, however, the pill-taking resulted in Mamaw's inadvertently dropping some of her powerful medication onto the floor, where it might at some point be picked up and swallowed by one of her toddler great-grandchildren, then a sterner lecture resulted, accompanied by a more spirited hymn, like "Rock of Ages." And on those occasions when Mamaw left an empty pan melting in flames into an eye of the stove, thereby posing a real threat to her life and Mom's house, and sending Mom into the Mother of All Scoldings, then Mamaw pulled out *the big guns*. All the neighbors came out of their houses to listen as "Onward, Christian Soldiers" — *and Mom* — bounced off the walls.

MY COUSIN RANDA LEE:
THE ULTIMATE TALK SHOW GUEST

M uch to my Aunt Gayleen's dismay, her baby girl Randa Lee is soon going to be the Nation's Most Wanted Talk Show Guest.

Randa Lee is our family's proverbial "black sheep," "skeleton in the closet," "Looney Tune," and any and all of the other terms that refer to someone with Randa Lee's (lack of) social graces. The rest of us in the family prefer to think that there was a terrible mix-up in the maternity ward of the Mobile General Hospital in 1950, and they just gave Aunt Gayleen the wrong baby. That's the only workable explanation we can come up with for this one-woman freak show named Randa Lee Guthrie.

We've all done our very best to keep her in that aforementioned closet. It's hopeless. Even the way she looks hasn't deterred her from seeking celebrity. For a woman with six toes on each foot, backward kneecaps, two rows of top teeth, and one nostril, she's remarkably proud of her appearance. And it's not just the way she looks that makes her certain she'll get on any, if not all, of the talk shows she wants to, she also has the following claims to fame:

- She, at age 48, is on her twenty-third husband — all of them dead now, Randa Lee maintains, of "natural causes." (Our mutual cousin, Brett, says it's because she made them actually consummate the marriage. Stranger things have happened — not *worse* things, of course, just *stranger* things.)

- She's had "half a sex change" — just on her left side. She couldn't decide whether she wanted to stay a woman or become the son her momma always wanted.

- She, herself, is the love child of a "Mars-man," and that's why she has so many abnormal physical characteristics. Her momma says she believes she'd remember if she (Aunt Gayleen) had ever had "marital relations" with someone from another planet. I tend to believe Aunt Gayleen on this one.

- Randa Lee says she was abducted one Friday night by her Mars-man daddy's family in the parking lot of the Boot Hill Launderette and Country/Western Nightclub, but they didn't keep her "but just for a couple of minutes." (Now that last part, I can certainly believe.)

- And, last but not least (and the one sure to get her on TV), she claims she gave birth to Elvis's "love child." From what I understand, Elvis didn't even drink, and he'd have had to be totally stinkoed to even get that close to a woman with one nostril. What's even weirder about this particular claim is that the child in question is only 15 years old. Elvis has been dead for more than 20 years. But, then again, Randa Lee does hang out an awful lot at Krispy Kreme Doughnuts and Burger "Kangs," spots of innumerable Elvis sightings.

Janelle, another cousin (who's President of the Mauverne, Alabama Chapter of the Jerry Springer Fan Club), warned Randa Lee that Jerry never books "solo" guests; but Randa Lee says she's totally prepared for the show's possible opposition to her being on there alone. She says she has actually learned how to beat herself up — literally. Not only can she pick herself up by the bra straps and throw herself out of her own chair, she can also blacken her own eyes and knock out her own teeth — both rows. She can also strangle herself, pull out large sections of her own hair, and cuss herself out. Those unique abilities make her perfect for Springer.

All the rest of us in the family, except Janelle, have already started packing. There's got to be somewhere in the Yukon where TV doesn't reach. Don'cha think?

I'M AGING LIKE FINE ... BALONEY

T he verb "age" is defined by Webster's New World Dictionary, in part, as "to make, or make seem, old or mature; to cause to ripen or become mature over a period of time under fixed conditions." The noun "process" is defined as (in part) "the course of being done," "a continuing development involving many changes," and "course, as of time." I prefer to think of both "aging" and "process" as something that happens to cheese — *not* something that happens to my body, face, and mind (although lately there hasn't been a whole lot of difference between Swiss cheese and my body, face, and mind).

Unfortunately, however, it does happen to humans. And if I ever just happen to forget (even for one rare, blessed, exquisite moment) that it (aging) is an ongoing (and extremely unrelenting) process, my teenaged daughters are always there to remind me.

"Mom, did you know that the mother of that really cute new boy in my Social Studies class is only 30 years old? That means that you're old enough to be *her* mom! Cool!"

"Mom, Lauren Black's mom said that you were wrong about those big brown spots on your hands. She said they're not freckles at all; they're *liver spots*, and that when people get to be *your* age, they just happen. She said it'll be *years and years* before she gets any."

For some reason, I still love those kids.

Of course, I could always go the way of Joan Rivers, Liz Taylor, Phyllis Diller, Michael Jackson, and others, and let vanity get the better of me. I could have reconstructive surgery, too. I could have my forehead de-furrowed, my under-eye area de-bagged, my upper lids de-puffed, my fuzzy upper lip stretched so that it doesn't look as if I've been a chain smoker since I was five years old; and I could de-gobblerize my supplemental chin (the one my children seem to find so charming in turkeys and certain lizards). Yes, I could certainly resort to any or all of these desperate measures — and I would, if it weren't for the fact that I pretty nearly faint from even the relatively slight pain that accompanies eyebrow tweezing. And, if that weren't enough, I've seen the results of Michael Jackson's abundant surgeries. That poor guy's face has been lifted, stretched, tucked, and bobbed so much it looks for all the world as if his belly button is now serving as his nose. It's about the same size. And if the physical suffering alone weren't enough to give me second thoughts about a face lift, the horror that I might end up looking even remotely like Michael does just might do the trick.

So, here I was fighting (and losing) "The Battle of the Facial Crevices."

As if the facial erosion weren't bad enough, it seems that we boomer women can no longer include shoulder bags as part of our wardrobe; they just seem to slide right off our sloping shoulders. And it's only now that I can finally understand why Katherine Hepburn chooses to wear turtlenecks in the heat of summer.

Our noses and ears get larger. Our lips disappear. Our eyelids sag, as do our bosoms, bellies, kneecaps, thighs, and butts.

And those are only the *physical* manifestations of age.

We aging baby boomers also have to face something even worse than that. We're "losing our cool." Just ask our kids. We dance funny; we listen to "elevator music" (The Doobie Brothers — *elevator music?*); we dress funny; we have no sense of humor; we're intolerant, inflexible, incontinent, and we know absolutely nothing. We can't see; we can't hear; and *everything* gives us gas.

And all this has happened so quickly. It seems like only yesterday I was a teenager, riding in the car with my mom, begging her to *please* let me change the radio station. I thought if I had to hear "My Way," "Everybody Loves Somebody Sometime," or "I Left My Heart in San Francisco" even one more time, I would surely die. Well, I guess it's true that what goes around comes around, because my kids do the same begging — only 35 years later, I'm driving around, happily listening to "the classics" — "Hotel California," "Inna-gadda-da-vida," and "Purple Haze," none of which could *ever* be described as "elevator music" -- except maybe for those versions I heard at the . . . *grocery store*!

Oh . . . my . . . GOSH! I *am* my momma!

MY ARMS AREN'T LONG ENOUGH
FOR ME TO READ THAT

There are so many facts of life my mom didn't touch on all those years ago when we had "that" talk. For instance, there was no mention of "Eye Failure at 40," which comes mainly in one of two forms: (1) myopia, i.e., nearsightedness; or (2) presbyopia, i.e., farsightedness. And I'm Presbyterian. Isn't that a co-inky-dink? My husband is nearsighted, but so far we haven't been able to find a Myopian church.

Not being a Myopian, I can neither relate to nor describe the onslaught of that particular affliction. Presbyopia, on the other hand, I can talk about at length — arm's length, to be exact. With my onslaught of presbyopia, I realized that one's arms shrink (lengthwise, at least) with age. This reality hit me recently. Well, actually, it was a few years ago. Okay, it was *several* years ago — on my 40th birthday. I got a card in the mail from one of my best friends. I could see the cartoon character on the front of the card; but when I attempted to read the message or decipher the name of the sender, I hadn't a clue. After trying unsuccessfully, several times, to figure out what "Burnt witches yoga bull Pigbreath" really meant, I had to swallow my pride and take the card to my husband, with my tail tucked (figuratively, of course) between my legs. From him, the Myopian, I learned it actually read, "Best wishes, your 'bud,' Patricia." What a relief.

Still, vanity precluded me from seeking ophthalmologic aid.

Then came a note from the teacher on my kindergartner's schoolwork that read (I thought), "Why don't you just keep this moron at home?" I was ready to punch this woman's lights out until my husband, the Myopic, came home from work to translate for me: "Why can't all kids perform this well at school?" Well, I got three of the words right. The next day, I went to the eye doctor.

And this underarm dingle-dangle is another thing. It's not like I ever had wonderfully firm triceps; but it seemed that all of a sudden, I had developed these flaps between my armpits and elbows that — if I move my arms back and forth fast enough — can be used as both a fan to cool food too hot to eat and bellows to get a really raging fire going in the fireplace.

And just where does all this extra skin come from? Once I turned 30, I realized just what a dirty word "gravity" really is. I *hate* gravity. If I lived on the moon, I'd look 17. Instead, I've got this "force" pulling my knees to my toes, my waist to my knees, my chest to my waist, my chin to my chest, and my eyes to my chin. Full-figured women's "chest areas" create an even greater hazard — thanks to gravity. If you're over 40 and busty, you have to either wear a bra with industrial-strength straps or be *very* careful buckling your car's shoulder harness — or, in my cousin Deanna's (48 HHH) case, her *lap* belt.

Not only does this "getting-old" stuff wreak havoc on one's body, it doesn't do much for the old wardrobe, either. For instance, most of us "BMWs" (Broadening, Middle-aged Women), don't (or certainly shouldn't) invest any longer in (with reasons for not doing so following each):

- anything sleeveless (underarm dingle-dangle)
- mini-skirts, skorts, shorts (fat knees and varicose veins the size of the Amazon River)
- bikinis/thong bathing suits (belly overhang and alligator butt)
- cut-off tops (jellybelly)
- leggings (thunder thighs)
- anything spandex (need you even ask?)
- thigh-high hose (danger of gangrene to the lower extremities)
- stirrup pants (we look like water buffalo in them)

The "In" items include:

- floor-length girdles
- turtleneck, long-sleeved, ankle-length bathing suits
- control-top, turtleneck support hose
- tunics, caftans, and muumuus
- boat covers
- canvas gazebos

So, here I am — gaining weight *and* fighting (and losing) "The Battle of the Facial Crevices."

At one frantic and momentous period in my life, when I especially desired to take 20 years off my face in 20 minutes, I found myself resorting to using the face-stretching, mucilage substance that tightened, tugged, and dragged my wrinkles into my hairline, and froze my face into what the manufacturer intended, I suppose, to be a smile. Unfortunately, in my case, on this all-important night, I looked less like a debutante than a middle-aged woman experiencing a "Where-will-you-be-when-your-laxative-starts-working?" moment.

Speaking of which, now, I suppose with all the urgency nutritionists are placing upon the need to increase fiber in our diets, the hemorrhoid treatment business is in the doldrums. That seems to explain why there's such a push all of a sudden to get us aging baby-boomers to use them to shrink the bags under our eyes. It's not that I doubt the cosmetic benefits to be derived from using these products for aesthetic purposes; it's just that if someone came up to me and said, "My goodness, Rebel! You look ten years younger! What *is* your secret?," I'd be somewhat reluctant to respond, "Why, thank you very much. I owe it all to my hemorrhoid medication."

PLEASE DON'T CALL ME *GRANDMA*!

I t's still a rather rude awakening for me when I'm around old (figuratively speaking) friends whom I haven't seen in a long time, and hear them refer to their "grandchildren." It's too much for me, the mother of 14- and 15-year-old daughters, to realize that I graduated from high school and college with people who are old enough to be (gulp) *grandparents*!

I ran into Janet Blackwell, a high-school classmate, at the mall a few years ago. We hadn't seen each other in more than 25 years (she doesn't "do" class reunions). We were in the Disney Store, where I was purchasing the mandatory Lion King™ paraphernalia for my kids. Janet informed me that she, too, was doing the same thing.

"Well, how old are your children now? Are they with you?" I asked, imagining her little ones agonizing, as mine were, over whether to choose Simba, Nala, Timon, or Puumba goodies.

It was at that very moment that a child of approximately six years of age came up behind her and grabbed her hand.

"C'mon, Grandma!" she ordered. "You promised me a pair of Nala pajamas!"

"*Grandma*?" I asked, painfully aware, albeit too late, of the astonishment in my voice.

"Why, yes. This is Meagan, Amy's daughter. Has it been that long since you and I have seen each other?" asked Janet.

"I guess it has," I responded. "I thought she *was* Amy."

"Obviously, it has been a while," Janet said, smiling. "Meagan is my oldest grandchild."

"Your *oldest*?"

"Yes. Amy also has twin boys who are three now; and Jennifer has a five-year-old son and a two-year-old daughter," Janet proudly informed me.

"You have *five* grandchildren?" I managed to ask, thinking, "Say it ain't so. This is *Janet*! This is the same Janet who screamed at the TV with me when The Beatles were on 'The Ed Sullivan Show.' Surely she can't be old enough to be a *grandmother*! If *she's* old enough to be one, then that means that *I* . . . ."

"So, how many grandchildren do *you* have?" she asked, jolting me back to the 90s.

"Me? Oh, goodness! *Grand*children? No grandchildren! Nope, not any! Nary a grandchild! Just children — small, *young* children, they are. Nowhere *near* old enough to have children of their own. So, *no* grandchildren for me! None! Zero grand-children!" I stammered, realizing just how defensive and stupid I sounded — and *looked* — as I stood there making the international "zero" sign with my thumb and fingers.

"Well, bless your heart. Just hang in there! You'll have grandbabies before you know it," she reassured me.

"Can't wait," I lied.

It's not that I don't want to *ever* be a grandmother. It's just that I'm not ready at this point in my life. Heck, I went to a One Dog Night concert not long ago. I find "The Roadrunner" cartoons just as funny now as I did as a youngster. I still love to jump on trampolines and play with Silly Putty®. I drive with all my car windows down (weather permitting) and what's left of my hair blowing freely. It's the closest I can come to making a Corvette convertible out of the Mom-mobile.

I'm a teenager trapped in a middle-aged body! "Grandma" is a four-letter word to me! It's hard enough for me to accept the fact that the girls I roller-skated with, and didn't slumber at slumber parties with, and threw up with on the "Tilt-a-Whirl" are *grandmothers*! How did that happen so fast? Are they *all* grandmothers now? Are *they* the ones who stay at home now on Friday and Saturday nights, keeping their grandchildren so that their *own* children can go out to dinner, a movie and/or dancing? The latter is what *we're* supposed to be doing — that's what I *am* doing! My mother and mother-in-law are the only grand-mothers in my family. They *look* like grandmothers. They *act* like grandmothers. Well, I may very well *look* like one, but I don't *feel* like one; and I certainly don't *act* like one — and I'm sure as heck not ready to *be* one!

The fact that my daughters are only 14 and 15 helps. Add to that the fact that their father is bound and determined that they won't even date until they're 45. (We'll be in "The Home" by then, anyway, gumming our barbecued rib bones, and sleeping 18 hours a day; and, at the rate we're going now, won't be able to remember that we even *have* kids.)

So, I figure I've got at least 30 good years before some little person calls me the "G" word. Actually, I've already decided that I'm not going to let my . . . *them* call me the "G" word. I much prefer "The Queen Mother" or, even better, *"YOUR ROYAL HINEY."*

TV STAYS ON ALL NIGHT NOW?

O n a recent Friday night, my husband and I went out to dinner with another married couple who are good friends of ours. "Did y'all see 'Letterman' last night?" our friend Mark asked.

"*The Lettermen*?" I asked. "I didn't even know they were still together."

"What are you talking about?" Mark queried, puzzled.

"I'm talking about The Lettermen — the group from the '50s. I didn't even know they were still alive — much less performing together," I responded.

"*No*! Not *The* Letter*men*! Letter*man*! *David* Letter*man*!" Mark informed me, like I was from another planet or something.

"Oh. Isn't he the one with the mother who's the Olympics correspondent?" I asked, innocently enough.

"Well, yes. She *was* there," Mark's wife, Katy, replied. "But don't you even know who David Letterman is?"

"Doesn't it count that I know who his mom is?" I asked.

"David Letterman is, like, *the* late-night talk show host," Mark huffily notified me.

"Well, I disagree," I countered, equally huffily, "*I* think Johnny Carson is *the* late-night talk show host!"

"*Johnny Carson*?" Mark screamed, in total disbelief. "*Johnny Carson*! Johnny Carson retired *ten years ago*!"

"He did?" I asked, incredulously.

"Yes, he did," Katy said. "Actually, it's only been about *five* years, though. How could you possibly *not* have known that?"

"I guess I was asleep."

"Asleep?"

"Yeah." I replied. "We're always asleep by 10:00. Sometimes even 9:30."

"Why?" Mark questioned.

"Why not?" I countered. "We get up at 5:30 every morning, and I'm never ready to get up, even when I go to sleep at 9:30. How could I *possibly* stay up to watch The Lettermen and then get up to get the kids off to school on time?"

"Letter*man*! DAVID Letter*MAN*!" bellowed Mark.

"What*ever*," I responded, more than a little offended by his brusqueness.

What a *grouch*! Sounds to me like *somebody* needs some *sleep.*

YO! QUEENIE!
WHAT'S IN THAT DANG PURSE?

W hat *is* it with Queen Elizabeth and that *purse*? She can't
even go out on her balcony to wave to the commoners
without having that silly thing looped over her forearm. What's
she got in there, for crying out loud? The Crown Jewels? I don't
think they'd all fit. Baseball cards? Probably not. Spending
money, just in case she has a Big Mac Attack when she's out?
Possibly. Beefcake photos of Brad Pitt that she stole from the
Queen Mum? Now, *that* is a distinct possibility.

But, really, what *is* in there? Her kids are all grown now. It's
not like she has to carry bandages and antibiotic cream or tissue
travel packs for runny, little royal noses. Why does a queen even
need a purse? She's got all those people to carry things for her.
Now, if she carried a stylish envelope clutch or even a shoulder
bag, I could understand — you know, as an accessory to her outfit.
Somehow, though, stylish envelope clutches just don't seem to
coordinate very well with baby-blue polyester, double-knit suits;
dog-ugly, sensible pumps; and whatever those things are that she
wears on her head. Could those be classified as *hats*? Besides,
she never carries clutches. It's always those grandma, snap-closed
purses with handles that one sees her carrying. I'd love to just
sneak a peek into one of them. I'd even be willing to trade peeks
with her. She could look into mine if she'd let me look into hers.
I have a feeling she'd be terribly disappointed. I mean, *I've* got all
those Brad Pitt beefcake shots to look forward to. All she's going
to find in my purse is used tissues (my baby girl has allergies);
several open packs of fuzzy chewable antacids (I love Polish
sausages; they don't love me); ticket stubs for "The Godfather";
receipts (circa early 1970s) for a Ginzu knife and a pet rock; an
ABBA eight-track; some fossilized chewing gum; a pair of
sunglasses with only one lens; two fuzz-covered lipsticks with no
tops; a 1976 Florida State University Student I.D. card; PTA
membership cards for the past several years (I may be a

disorganized slob, but I'm a good mother); four open bottles of dried-up nail polish; keys that open who-knows-what; an empty box of dental floss; seventy-six school pictures of my daughters; eleven capless ballpoint pens that no longer have any ink (it soaked into the lining of my purse long ago); a pacifier (which is extremely hard to explain since my youngest child is 14 years old now); and one very faded photo of what looks frightfully like Rodney Dangerfield (thankfully *not* beefcake).

What's even harder for me to understand than why the Queen of England feels the need to carry a purse is women who carry those clear plastic ones. These women obviously have a superiority complex — in addition to having no children younger than eighteen — and no heartburn. I was standing in line behind one of "them" the other day at the grocery store. There she was, with her white grapes, white wine, white meat, and white unscented toilet paper. Then she pulled her trimline wallet/ checkbook and non-leaking fountain pen out of her see-through purse. The only items remaining in there were a slender brush — with no hairs in it, a tube of lipstick with the top still on, a set of keys that probably all open something, and unused tissues — in their original package.

"That's a very nice purse," I commented, feeling somewhat magnanimous.

"Why, thank you; but I'm afraid it's a bit of a mess. I just haven't had a chance to clean it out," she replied.

I leaned on the scale while the cashier rang up her grapes.

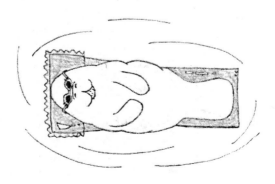

MY OTHER LIVES

I t's five minutes before noon on May 25th in Pensacola, Florida. According to the thermometer on my deck, it's 92° outside; and, according to my local television weatherperson, the humidity at this moment should be right at 98% — with an "up" arrow behind it. And my neighbor just ran down her driveway — the first installment on her daily five-mile jog.

I walked out to my mailbox in the front yard ("front yard," two words; "backyard," one word — can anyone explain that to me?) a few minutes ago, and was manifesting all the warning signs of a heat stroke by the time I got back into my 70° home.

Another neighbor once attempted to explain my lack of heat tolerance to me.

"You were a Viking's mistress in your first life," she imparted, with nary a smile on her face.

"I thought you said I was the mistress of an antebellum plantation," I responded, somewhat condescendingly, but not so much so that it would hurt her feelings. She's really serious about this reincarnation thing. In fact, she's the President of the Pensacola Chapter of the Shirley MacLaine Fan Club. She's also its Vice-President, Secretary, Treasurer, Sergeant-at-Arms, and only card-carrying member. Reincarnation's not real big in the Bible Belt.

"I *did*, and you *were*," she said.

"Well, then," I continued, "wouldn't I have developed at least a little heat tolerance living in Georgia in the mid-1800s? I mean, what with no air-conditioning and those pantaloons and all?"

"You would have if you'd been born and raised in the South, or even if you had spent much time here," was her rational response.

"Well, *wasn't* I — and *didn't* I?" I humored her.

"Heavens, *no*! I *swear*! You just *kill* me! Don't you remember *anything* at all from that time?" she asked, totally dumfounded at my lack of memory for things that happened over 130 years ago. "In that particular life, you were born in *Ireland*! When you were 15, you met Samuel Beaujois, a landed gentleman from Jonesboro, Georgia, who was in Dublin on cotton business. Y'all were married two weeks after you met, and he brought you back to Georgia to live on his plantation. You did fine there for the first six months — 'til May came around. Then your husband got so tired of your ceaseless whining about the heat and mosquitoes and gnats and no-see-'ums that he took you all the way back to Dublin himself and left you there. And that's the only lifetime you've ever lived where you had any exposure whatsoever to heat and humidity — until this one. Unless, of course, you count the time you and Napoleon spent those two weeks in August in the South of France."

"Oh, yeah. I keep forgetting about that. But now please tell me again about me and Jack Nicklaus. I just *love* that particular life," I teased, although the joke, as always, went right over her head.

"It wasn't you and *Jack Nicklaus*! It was you and *Tsar Nicholas* — of Russia!" she screamed, totally frustrated.

"Oh — sorry. I'm always getting those two guys mixed up. What kind of golfer was the tsar, anyway? Seems to me I recall that he was nowhere near as good as Jack. Better-looking, mind you; but that *slice* of his!"

"You're absolutely hopeless, you know that?" she surrendered, hastily leaving my presence.

"Which *life*?" I shouted after her, barely able to contain my laughter.

I hope that didn't sound too mean. I'm going to try to be much nicer — perhaps when I come back as Goo-Ra, Amazon Queen of Venus.

HAVE THEY STARTED CLONING HUSBANDS YET?

I t seems that nearly every time I get together with certain of my married women friends, I'm reminded (by them) of what a remarkable husband I have — especially in comparison with theirs. It's not that they don't love the men they married; it's just that . . . well, according to them, their spouses could all use some instruction in the fine (and apparently *dying*) art of considerate husbandhood. The major topic of conversation at our last get-together was their husbands' inability to recognize the purpose of a clothes hamper.

I certainly don't have anything to complain about in the "clothes hamper" area, especially compared to Janet. Her husband walks in the front door of their home every day after work, already half undressed. His coat is on his arm. His tie is in his mouth, and he's tearing at the buttons on his shirt. By the time he's made it to their bedroom, he's left his coat and tie on the living room floor, his shirt on the sofa, one shoe on the recliner, another on the TV, one sock on the coffee table, another hanging from a light fixture, and his slacks on the stationery bike. Janet, with good reason, isn't the least bit turned on by this undressing routine. To the contrary, she's well aware of the fact that this is *not* a prelude to an afternoon of wild and crazy "stuff." It is simply her husband's clothes-changing routine. Janet claims that this has been his practice every single day he's worked since they've been married. His momma always picked up after him before he got married. Why, he inquires, should things be any different now?

Why, indeed.

But that's not the problem Jackie has with *her* husband. He doesn't leave his clothes lying around all over the house. Jackie *wishes* that were his shortcoming. No, her Brian at least waits until he gets into their bathroom to change clothes; and it's there that he leaves the cast-offs of his workaday world — in a pile on their bathroom floor, *two feet* from the laundry hamper. And while she does wish that he were more thoughtful and would actually place his clothes *in* the hamper, that's not what really bothers her. That would have to be that as soon as he changes into his sweats or gym shorts, he heads straight for the living room sofa, whereupon, in his favorite position (horizontal), with remote control in hand, he begins watching the cable sports channels. He lies there and snaps his fingers at Jackie for drink orders (one snap for coffee, two for beer, three for cola). The television stays on until Jackie gently wakes him around midnight so that he can come to bed.

In the first place, I'd bend those snapping fingers of his backwards until his fingernails touched his wrist the first time he "summoned" me with them. Secondly, I don't think "gently" is the adverb that would appropriately describe how I'd wake him if he did that to *me* night after night.

Les, my husband, was "raised right," as we from the South are so inclined to say. This is a man who doesn't even begin to shed his "corporate image" until he's reached our closet. Once there, he stuffs his dirty shirt into the overflowing hamper. He then hangs his slacks on his allotted twelve inches of closet rod, unless they need to be dry cleaned — in which case he can either put them in *his* car and take them to the dry cleaners the next day; *or* he can put them in *my* car alongside the Nehru jackets, leisure suits, and polyester bell-bottoms he gave me to take to the cleaners . . . a while back.

He then stacks his shoes neatly on top of his others in his allotted twelve inches of closet floor space. Then he hangs up his coat and tie, and puts his change and wallet on his chest of drawers.

After he's changed into his "post"-office gear, he even helps me get dinner on the table. This consists primarily of attempting to pry the mystery meat loose from the pan, scraping the bottoms of the rolls, transferring the lump of rice/meat/beans/potatoes (all interchangeable) into a bowl, and filling the glasses with ice for the blackened tea I've prepared.

He's *such* a good boy.

(Cloning terms negotiable. All major credit cards accepted.)

WOMEN'S DIRECTIONS

I f you're trying to get me to drive from Point A to Point B, *please* don't tell me, "Drive south about 325 yards, then turn north-northwest, and proceed in that direction for another 267 feet." I'll never even back out of my driveway. I need to hear: "Turn right at the end of your street. Then drive about as far as it is from that hardware store with the monkey wrench sign to the skating rink; then go left about as far as it is from that new Moo-Burger on Limbaugh Lane to where that lunatic florist is who does all those tacky pompom mums for the high schools' homecoming games. You know, the one who gets so many of her orders mixed up. She's the one who sent the *'With Deepest Sympathy'* arrangement to Jenny Johnson when she had her fifth son, and the *'Congratulations'* arrangement to Monroe Eudecker when he got sent up for embezzlement, and the *'Get Well Soon!'* to poor LouDell Moorhead's momma's funeral."

Now, those are *my* kind of directions — "women's" directions. Those yards and feet and compass points are "men's" directions; they mean absolutely *nothing* to me, or to most other women, for that matter.

The very last thing *I* want to hear if I have absolutely no idea *whatsoever* where I'm going is, "Head south on 29-A. Take that for maybe five-and-a-quarter miles. Then turn east-southwest. Go about 320 — no 322 — yards to the fork in the road. Bear south-west-east until you reach a dead end. Turn north-north-south there. Our house is 163.7 feet down on the north-southwest corner curve." Yeah, right — like I keep my compass and yardstick with me at all times.

I'd be inclined, at that point, to ask Mr. Magellan to put his wife, Sue Ellen Magellan, on the phone. She'd say something like:

"Okay, hon, now from your house, you're gonna go like you're going to that little 'Chitlins & Sushi' restaurant that burned down last summer — only don't go quite that far. Just before it, turn by that discount fabric store that doesn't even carry peau de soie, but they do sell all their patterns at half-price, but so does Wal-Mart; so I usually buy all mine there, anyway, because it's closer. Where was I? Oh, yeah. Okay, then go on down past that house with all the washing machines and refrigerators and stuff in the front yard, and keep on going 'til you get to that triple-wide with the car engines hangin' from the trees; turn right — I think — there and just keep on going past Doc Watson's house. Did you know he's not even a doctor? I have no idea why he's even *called* 'Doc,' unless it's because his wife has those two really long front teeth, and she's always asking everybody, 'What's up?' And she *does* look an awful lot like Bugs Bunny, so maybe that's why. It's the only reason I can think of. Besides, if he were a *real* doctor, you'd think she'd be able to afford to get those teeth filed down by now, wouldn't you? And they'd certainly be able to afford a nicer house. You know what I mean? You haven't seen it? Oh, honey! It would gag a *maggot*! It's a hideous, Pepto-Bismol® pink, adobe-looking thing — sort of a retro/Alamo, I guess is what they were shooting for. And it has a *brown* roof! Can you *believe* that? I can't even *imagine* a pink house; but if I had to have one, I'd certainly not put a *brown* roof on it! *Or* a black one. That's like 50's Elvis — pink and black. Did I ever tell you my freshman art instructor gave me an 'F' on a two-shade painting I did just because I used pink and black? He hated Elvis with an absolute passion. Personally, I think it was because he was jealous. He was a little, bitty, ol' thing with, like, eleven orange hairs on his big, ol' watermelon of a head. And, poor thing, his feet were no bigger than mine — and I wore a four-and-a-half back then. And, from what I understand, little feet on a man are *not* a good thing, if you know what I mean. And I'm sure Elvis wore at least a thirteen, even if he did have absolutely *hideous* taste in clothes — *and* hair. Surely, you saw how Priscilla wore hers at their wedding. Well, honey, that was *his* idea. All I know is she must've really loved him, to have been seen in public looking like a *vampire hooker* — and with three pairs of false eyelashes on! He was really gorgeous back then, but I'd have loved to have gotten hold of him and washed that hairspray and dye and grease out of his hair. And I'd have *burned* those white jumpsuits and capes, and put that man in a double-breasted Armani suit and Gucci loafers. But, then, that wouldn't have been Elvis, would it? The man *was* a hunka, hunka burnin' love, regardless of what he wore. No wonder poor little Mr. O'Casey hated him so much he gave me that 'F.' I really detested him for a long time for that — Mr. O'Casey, *not* Elvis. I loved *him* — Elvis, *not* Mr. O'Casey, although I was much more into The Beatles and Stones. Anyway, I'd never use those two colors together now. Gray would be the only color roof I'd *ever* put on a pink house — as if anything in the world could help *that* house besides maybe a Molotov cocktail.

Well, I guess there's just no accounting for taste. If you could see his wife, you'd know what I mean. Her hair is as red as Delbert Cheeseman's neck, and she wears it in a *ponytail!* Can you *believe* that? And she's 60 years old, if she's a day — with a *ponytail!* And she wears these acrylic nails that are at least an inch long — with all those little gold charms of playing cards imbedded in them. Honey, I'm telling you, if she's ever sitting in her car at a red light, doing any, shall we say, 'nasal grooming,' and she gets rear-ended, she's gonna give herself a frontal lobotomy! Actually, that just might benefit society, you know.

"But, anyway . . . where was I? Oh, yeah — directions. So, once you pass their house, if you're still able to drive, what with the nausea and all from having been subjected to that *bodacious* mess, just keep going on down that road. Pretty soon — maybe five or ten or fifteen . . . or twenty minutes — I don't know — something like that — I've never timed it; anyway, just keep going on down that road. You'll see that colossal white house that looks like Tara from 'Gone With the Wind,' which is my absolute favorite movie in the entire world. I just loved Vivien Leigh as Scarlett O'Hara. Did you realize that her full name was Katie Scarlett O'Hara Hamilton Kennedy Butler? What a mouthful! Nowadays, I guess she'd have it all hyphenated to be politically correct. But you know what I don't understand? Why in this world did they ever get *Leslie Howard* to play Ashley? He looked as out of place as a maxi-pad commercial in a Super Bowl game! He reminds me so much of Haywood Bonesteel down at the bank — skinny, blonde, wimpy. That's probably why Haywood's wife Claudelle has been seen so many nights at the club with Eldon Hinote. You might not know Eldon yet. He's *not* one of us, you know. He's from up around Birmin'ham. He's not all that much to look at — he's certainly *no* Clark Gable, I can tell you *that* much; but he does at least stand up to Claudelle like Haywood would never begin to do. Not that I blame him. She's the meanest, little, ol' thing. She's like a pit bull in a Pomeranian's body. She's broken poor little Haywood's nose at least three times. She says his personal trainer did it, teaching him kickboxing; but we all know better.

"Oh, goodness, what *was* I talking about? Oh, yeah — the big white house. You haven't seen it? Well, *that,* darlin', is Tammy Jo Pigg's mansion. You'll just *die* when you see it! But, honey, it took her *three* marriages to get that house! The first one was for love, but evidently *not* for love of *poverty,* so she divorced him after a year, and married what *she* thought was money. It seems that's also why *he* married *her.* They each thought the other had money, when actually neither of them had two nickels to rub together. *That* marriage lasted until the first bank statement came in the mail. So, then, Tammy Jo found out that rich, old Mr. Pigg's wife Ileta had died. Can you believe that — *Ileta Pigg*! *What a hoot!* Could've been worse, though. What if she'd married Bob *Carr*? Well, anyway, Tammy Jo wasted no time in paying a condolence call on the poor widower; and the rest, as they say, is history. So there she is, in that magnificent house, with a husband permanently attached to an oxygen tank. That being the case, I imagine she doesn't have to worry too much about 'you know what.' I *know* she has to be *grateful* for that! I saw Mr. Pigg last month in Dr. Threadgill's office when I took Momma in for her check-up. He looked like he died two years ago.

"But surely Tammy Jo has her own bedroom. Wouldn't you think? Shoot, I'd make absolutely sure *that* stipulation made it into the prenuptial agreement.

"Anyway, what was I getting at? Oh, directions! Okay, so you just keep going on down that road 'til it dead-ends. Speaking of dead-ends, did you hear that Claire Sayer's husband lost his tenure at the university, and had to take a job cleaning out *porta-potties*?"

Granted, this might sound like the most drawn-out way possible to learn how to get from one point to another, but with these vivid, picturesque "women's" directions, I'm sure to find my way to where I'm going — provided I can ever get on my way.

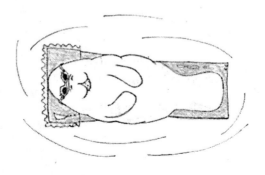

RATING SHOPPING FOR VIOLENCE

L ast week I got together with some of my married women friends, as we do every so often, to exchange marriage "war" stories. The subject of our latest get-together was our husbands' going to the movies with "The Boys" (with which we absolutely do *not* have a problem). Our problem was with the subject matter of the movies they all seem to live for. The Boys, for reasons I can't begin to comprehend, anxiously anticipate every single Jean Claude Van Damme, Steven Segal, Arnold Schwartzenegger, Sylvester Stallone, and Bruce Willis punch-your-face-off-and-kick-and-stomp-you movie that comes to town. For reasons that totally escape their wives, they simply love that savagery. Maybe they're living out their fantasies vicariously through these "action heroes." I don't know what the big deal is. I've told Les a million times that he can see more action — *live*, at that — if he'd just accompany me to the mall the day after Thanksgiving.

I recall one particular incident that would make Arnold and Sly and all those other walking testosterone-overloads tremble like Chihuahuas. From what I could gather from the sketchy information given me after the paramedics left, two women both simultaneously spotted and grabbed the last 75%-off, plus-size stretch pants on the rack. Onlookers reported that a particularly gruesome fight ensued, with neither woman willing to relinquish custody of the pants, which, after nearly 20 minutes of nonstop tugging, had been stretched to approximately twice their original size (they *were* stretch pants, after all). It was, according to eyewitnesses, a frightful thing to behold — acrylic fingernails flying everywhere, amid blows inflicted by purses estimated to weigh no less than fifty pounds each. Thankfully, there were no serious injuries to either woman. Unfortunately, the diminutive security officer who attempted to break up the altercation was rendered momentarily unconscious after being squished between the two overzealous shoppers. As for the pants, ... Well, it seems they were too large for either "contender" after all the pulling and yanking that accompanied the battle for them. But, as it turns out, once stretched, they were a perfect fit for the wee security officer's wife.

I keep telling Les what he's missing by choosing not to go shopping with me on this — "The Shopping Day From Hell." Whatever it is that gets these macho men's violence adrenaline flowing pales in comparison to two women grabbing the last 75%-off sale item.

Arnold *Shmarnold*. He'd never stand a chance at the mall.

HURRY BACK, SHAG CARPETING

A lthough I would be the first to admit my appreciation for the demise of harvest gold and avocado kitchen appliances — along with Mediterranean and Spanish red velvet sofas, cable spool coffee tables, and black velvet Elvis "portraits" — I'm at a complete loss as to understanding what kind of sick, sadistic doofus would declare shag carpeting a decorating "no-no." It was probably some *man* who has never spent even one moment on his hands and knees — ice cube, case knife, and tweezers all going at once — trying to get a rapidly-growing wad of hot pink bubble gum out of one-half-inch-long, champagne beige carpeting. Then there's the dog wee, baby barf, "buh-sketti sauce," knee blood, grape juice, chili, fish scales, watermelon, and on and on, ad infinitum. Those stains and holes are with you — and are a direct reflection *on* you for as long as you own that carpet. You can't hide them, or even begin to cover all of them. There in those carpet scars lies your family's history, in conspicuous, if somewhat faded, shapes and colors — Bile Green, Dog Wee Yellow, Old-Blood Brown, Fermented- and Unfermented-Grape-Juice-Maroon, and others ranging in hue from "Some-Moron-Spilled-the-Clorox White" to "Volcanic, Fireplace-Cinder, Black-Hole Black."

Twenty-five years ago, we needed only to cut the offending stain out of the depths of that three-inch-long variegated red, gold or green shag carpeting. Even cinder holes vanished with an expert cut-and-paste job.

One didn't even have to vacuum more than once a year if one didn't want to. All it took was just a wooden shag rake to make that matted carpet look shaggy again. I always likened that "picking and lifting" process to what my Aunt Clorette does to her hair with her hair pick after she gets it "set" at LaVon's Beauty, Nail & Knick-Knack Galleria. She's had a standing appointment with LaVon at 7:30 on Friday mornings since January of 1961, when Jackie Kennedy became First Lady. She took a picture of Jackie that was in Ladies Home Journal to LaVon, and, pointing at Jackie, told LaVon "That is *exactly* what I want to look like." Well, LaVon was a good beautician, but even *she* knew she was no miracle worker. She realized it was going to take more than a modified pageboy hairdo and a pillbox hat to make Aunt Clorette look "exactly" like Jackie Kennedy. For one thing, Aunt Clorette had a set of teeth that entered a room several seconds before the rest of her body got there. She also had what certain folks in our family called (not to her face, of course) a "uni-brow." It was just one great, long, wild and fuzzy eyebrow with absolutely no break whatsoever over her nose. As if that weren't bad enough, it seems that her sister, my Aunt Vora Lee, cut off all of Aunt Clorette's eyelashes when she (Clorette) was two years old; and they never grew back. So now she's got this uni-brow thing directly above these coal-black, bug eyes with nary a trace of an eyelash. And her eyes kind of "go off" in different directions, sort of like a Pekingese dog's do. And then there's her nose. Well, the story has it that when Aunt Clorette was about three years old, Aunt Vora Lee swatted at a mosquito on Aunt Clorette's nose. Aunt Vora Lee claims that she was only trying to keep the mosquito from biting her little sister, which is, on the surface, a pretty nice thing to do; only she was using their daddy's work boot to do it. This was back in the 20's, and they lived in a little, bitty town in south Alabama. The doctor there set her nose as best he could; but she was left looking pretty much like a duck-billed platypus. Consequently, she didn't walk out of that beauty shop looking *anything* like Jacqueline Bouvier Kennedy, except for her hair. In the bouffant arena, LaVon is considered an "artiste."

Out of respect and admiration for Jackie, Aunt Clorette wore her hair just like Jackie's up until the very day she (Jackie, not Aunt Clorette) married Aristotle Onassis. Aunt Clorette had one of her "hissy fits" when Jackie did that. It was on that very day that she called LaVon for an emergency appointment, and it was also on that very day that she started wearing it in what LaVon calls the "Upside-Down-Eiffel-Tower-French-twist." She still wears it that way.

It is a very *tall* hairstyle. That hair, as a matter of fact, makes up nearly one-fourth of Aunt Clorette's total height. She's only about 4'9" tall, and getting shorter every year. But somehow her hair keeps getting taller and taller with each day that passes after her Friday appointment. By Tuesday morning, that lacquer hairspray has literally "become one" with her head, forcing her teased and shellacked mountain of hair upward, making it look not at all unlike a lavender-gray, hairy polyurethane football perched on top of her head. And, as much as it distresses our family, there is absolutely *nowhere* she *won't* go looking like that. There've been sightings of her at Piggly Wiggly, Target, and even, heaven forbid, at the *mall*. I'm afraid we're talking no pride here. Yet, strangely enough, this is a woman who wouldn't be caught dead in a pair of jeans, even though she wears a size two. And she won't even wear slacks; she wears "lounge sets" or "lounging pajamas." She wears nothing on her feet except obscenely expensive Italian shoes. She had to stay in bed for three days, *heavily sedated*, when she found out that it wasn't a joke that her Charity League was going to raise money for the homeless by modeling fashions from (get out the smelling salts) . . . a *discount* store. That's why it's so hard to imagine that this is the same woman who leaves home daily, from Tuesday through Friday morning at 7:30, looking more and more with each passing day like a little, hairy scud missile.

Be afraid, Sadam. Be *very* afraid.

THE NEW L.S.D.

B ack in the late 60's (my formative years), those years of
Beatles, Stones, and Hendrix; the years of "Tune in, turn
on, drop out," and long before "Just Say No," we teenagers
were bombarded by drug terms, one of which was "L.S.D.,"
or "l(y)s(ergic acid)d(iethylamide)," a drug that produced
hallucinations similar to those taking place during a psychotic
state. One of the most dangerous side effects of this drug was
that it induced many of its users to take off all their clothes in
public at huge rock concerts in places like Woodstock, New
York — particularly users like Nadine the Cellulite Queen from
Kushla, Alabama, who should never expose their nakedness to an
unsuspecting crowd, regardless of (or perhaps *because of*) the
psychotic state of said crowd.

Well, it appears that these particular initials, L.S.D., have been
replaced in the United Kingdom by "Lottery Stress Disorder."
According to Dr. Robert Hunter, a psychiatrist at the Gartnavel
Royal Hospital in Glasgow, he has "discovered an outbreak of
lottery-losers suffering from 'deflation of mood and feelings of
hopelessness' leading to inebriation."

Translation: They get drunk every time they fail to become
instant millionaires.

Dr. Hunter goes on to say, "We have noted several cases of
this compulsive behavior in the clinic and are at a loss to know
how to help the sufferers." Well, a good, swift kick in the rump
might help. What a bunch of babies! Did they not ever get the
old "Who said 'Life is fair?'" speech from their mommas?

Dr. Hunter, in his imminent wisdom, goes on to say, "We have
given the condition the provisional name of Lottery Stress
Disorder, or L.S.D."

Well, in the first place, Dr. Hunter, "L.S.D." has already been
taken — as has "P.M.S." So why don't you just call a shovel a
shovel, and give the "disorder" the name it deserves, "CBS" — or
"Cry-Baby Syndrome?" In other words: Nobody likes a whiner.
If you ain't got it to lose, don't risk it. Don't go around thinking the
world owes you something. If you're gonna dance, you gotta pay
the piper. Money can't buy happiness. And, most importantly,
who's to say that if you won all that money, you wouldn't end up
just like Howard Hughes — a paranoid, stinky, old hermit with
three-inch toenails?

Meanwhile, Dr. Lawrence Price, a psychiatrist at Yale

University, says the syndrome does not exist in lottery-crazed America. He states, "Our population has become desensitized to the kind of stress Hunter is describing. It probably speaks to the rarified British atmosphere that a stress of this sort can provoke such dramatic symptoms."

Exceptions do exist, however, right here in the good old U.S. of A.

My cousin Linda's next-door neighbor's mother-in-law's best friend's husband's uncle, Dewey DeWayne Darden, stayed drunk for nearly a week after having lost the Florida Lottery the last time it got up to over $50 million. It wasn't so much the "deflation of mood" or even "the feeling of hopelessness" experienced by the *rarified* British that led to Dewey's prolonged inebriation. It was more the "fear for his life" when he realized there was *no way* he could *ever* explain to his wife Merleece that he had hocked her momma's heirloom silver tea set to get the $1,000 he had bet on the lottery. You see, Merleece is a very large, very *mean* woman with a hair-trigger temper. Dewey, on the other hand, cries over those Taster's Choice® coffee commercials, agonizes over "The Young and the Restless," wears clothes from the Sears' Boys' Department, and dresses up as Barney Fife every single year for his V.F.W.'s Annual TV Star Costume Party; and he always wins the award for Best Likeness, even though Barney was probably a good 30 pounds heavier than Dewey.

Well, after *not* winning the lottery, Dewey was so scared to tell Merleece about her momma's tea set that once he sobered up, he got two Sheriff's Deputies to be with him while he told her. (He tried to get the entire Sheriff's Posse, but they wouldn't agree to that, even though they all know how mean that woman can be.) However, Merleece was uncharacteristically calm when Dewey broke the news to her. As a matter of fact, she even served sugar cookies and coffee to the deputies. Then, when they left, she folded little Dewey like an accordion, and stuffed him into the clothes hamper. Then she closed the lid, and sat on it for a very, very, *very* long time.

So now Dewey has the distinction of being the first American diagnosed with L.S.D.; but in his case, it stands for "Living *Scared to Death*."

PLEASE DON'T DRESS
LIKE THAT DOWN HERE

O ne of the very few — extremely rare — *bad* things about summer in Florida isn't the heat. This *is* Florida, after all; heat is expected. And it's not even the humidity. That's expected, too. No, the single worst thing about living in Florida in the summertime is the inevitability of seeing Eunice and Lew Bjorklund (formerly of Green Bay, Wisconsin) in their clothes. I'm not saying that it would be okay to see them *without* their clothes — not by any means. I don't know, however, that it could be much worse than seeing them dressed.

I'm fairly certain everyone living in Florida has a Eunice and Lew living within a five-mile radius of his or her home.

Eunice and Lew retired two years ago; and, after having spent every vacation in Florida for the past 22 years, decided that this land of sugar white sand and 98% average summer humidity was where they wanted to spend the "winter of their lives" — and the springs, summers, and falls. And that's great. They're really nice, quiet, law-abiding citizens — until they come out of their house. That's when so many of us are made even more aware of the crucial need for Fashion Police or anyone who could legally detain people like Eunice and Lew, and hold them in protective custody while imposing upon them a mandatory fashion rehabilitation sentence.

You see, Eunice and Lew could very easily be the poster couple for the Terminally Tacky, if that affliction were ever classified, as it should be, as a true "condition."

Eunice comes out every year at about the same time azaleas and dogwoods do — mid-March — in what might be described as a "Tasteless Woman Retiree in Florida Ensemble," i.e., a sleeveless, ruffled blouse (of course, Eunice pronounces it so that it rhymes with "house"; I and all my kin have always rhymed it with "cows"), black polyester lace-trimmed shorts (circa 1969), brown suede Hush Puppies, and, of course, the pièce de résistance, suntan knee-high hose.

Having been born and raised in the South (always, please, with a capital "S"), I'm not about to be disrespectful to anyone my momma's age or older. Consequently, when I see Eunice planting her bushes and trees in her spring ensemble (at least a full month before the rest of us are anywhere near ready to don shorts), I always say, "Nice outfit, Mrs. Bjorklund." And, as always, she responds, "Thank you. It's new."

Uh-huh. Just like my white, vinyl go-go boots.

This outfit is bad enough for someone who has spent three hours a day for five months in a tanning bed, but when you put black polyester shorts on legs that haven't seen sunlight in six months, and with varicose veins the size of jumper cables, believe me, it ain't a pretty sight.

But, then, Eunice pales in comparison with Lew. Lew really has to be seen to be appreciated — but I'll do my best.

Back in the 1960's, Lew, with his unerring eye for the trends of the future, could foresee the run there would be on plaid, double-knit shorts in the 90's, so he bought 80 pairs. And when he pairs those pairs of plaid double-knit shorts with his investment in madras shirts (also from the 60's), well, then we have "Plaidras."

And, of course, when in Rome . . . , so Lew has brown leather sandals — very Floridian — which he wears with black knee-high socks and garters — very *South* Floridian. And then there's that little white expanse between where the plaid shorts end and the black knee-high socks begin — totally blinding.

Unfortunately, their fashion faux pas (pases?) don't end the third week in September. They also have fall and winter "outfits." On any given December morning, one can see Lew in his warm-up suits or sweatsuits, worn — *always* — with wing-tip shoes.

And then there's Eunice — decked out in the "I LOVE BOB BARKER" sweatsuit she bought 30 pounds ago, when she and Lew went to Los Angeles for a vacation and the once-in-a-lifetime opportunity to appear on "The Price Is Right." For whatever reason, Eunice wasn't chosen to be a contestant. She still swears it was because Lew told the interviewers she had just finished off five margaritas before they got in line.

The last thing in the world I want to do is offend any *tasteful* Northerners who choose to either visit or live in the South — and there are many. It's just that there's also a vast plethora of Eunices and Lews, for whom I feel there is a definite need for a 12-step program: "Hi, I'm Eunice, and I have *no* taste whatsoever" or "Hi, I'm Lew, and I dress like this on purpose."

Granted, there are also Southerners who would be well served by the same type of program. For instance, there are those inevitable Southern talk-show guests who feel the need to go on national television to air their embarrassing lifestyles. As if it's not bad enough to even appear on these trashy talk shows, you feel you must divulge to the entire world that you are your father's girlfriend; or that you're addicted to the Home Shopper's Club to the extent that you've lost your husband, your children, and your will to live; or that you went to the Junior Prom with your granddaughter's boyfriend. But even that's not enough for you! You have to appear on national television wearing *white* shoes (in *December*) with *black* hose! This is *so* humiliating for the rest of us! Have you no pride, woman? No shame at all? Have you not learned anything in your 40+ years of life in the South? Any self-respecting Southern woman, first of all, does not *ever* wear white shoes after Labor Day (and the growing consensus is that they shouldn't even be worn *at all.*) Secondly, she never, never, *never* wears hose that are darker than her shoes. What is the matter with these women? They know the rules! No white shoes after Labor Day; no black shoes on or after Easter -- except, of course, black patent leather. What could be easier than that?

Turnabout's fair play, I hear. It seems that Elmer Dee and Betty Lou Turnipseed have moved their "double-wad" (double-wide) trailer from Skeeter Creek, Mississippi to Green Bay, where Betty Lou wears tank tops and spandex stirrup pants with stilettos, and Elmer Dee wears his "I Seen Elvis at the Burger King" T-shirt and the "bubba" cap that reads "I got a gun for my wife — GOOD TRADE!"

Well, we got Eu and Lew for Elmer Dee and Betty Lou — *REALLY* GOOD TRADE!

WEIRDO MAGNETS

M y husband and I have always been sort of "Weirdo Magnets." No matter where we've been, or where we go, even if there's just us and *one other person* in some place like the Superdome, that other person is going to be weird. And he or she is going to find us, is going to sit with us, and is going to want to be a part of our lives for-eh-ver. Sort of like "Fatal Attraction," but without the sex and the boiled pet rabbit.

Case in point: In the summer of 1983, or, as we prefer to call it, "1 B.C." (Before Children), Les and I awoke early one morning, and headed out to the Intracoastal Waterway, which runs inland and parallel to Pensacola Beach, in anticipation of having a little "private time" before the mob descended upon us. That private time was short-lived, however. We had been relaxing on our inflatable floats for about ten minutes when seemingly out of nowhere, over the dunes, came the loudest, largest family of six I had ever seen. They came bearing coolers (four of them) full to the brim; overflowing, grocery bags (eight of them); and a very concave *innerspring mattress.*

From what we could tell, it was Daddy, Momma, and their four young'uns. And although there was a roughly 40-mile stretch of beach for them to sprawl out on, they homesteaded (surprise, surprise) no more than 20 feet from the *Weirdo Magnets.*

Les and I just looked at each other, hung our heads, tried really hard not to cry, and paddled on our floats farther down the shoreline and, we thought, out of harm's way. But then, to our horror, since voices carry so far over the water, we heard the following:

"*Hooo wheee*, Momma! Look at them purdy floats them people's on out there in the water!"

"Ooh, them *is* nice, son! They look like tin foil, what with all that silver colorin' an' all! I ain't never seen none that nice afore!"

"Momma, can me and the others go ast them people can we play on their floats?"

"Why, shore, Junior! Just ast *nice.*"

It was at that point that Les and I began to paddle harder, *much* harder. It was no good. The wind was against us and behind Junior and the other "Young'uns From Hell." They were on us like piranhas in a kiddie pool in less than a minute-and-a-half. We knew we were goners. They outnumbered us, outweighed us, and obviously had outsmarted us. There was nothing left for us to do but surrender our floats to them, and walk the cowards' walk back to the beach.

From there, we had a perfect view of Junior and his siblings enjoying *our* floats. But even *their* joy was short-lived. Within ten minutes, Momma and Daddy were out there pulling their kids off so that they (Momma and Daddy) could lay claim to the comfort of *our* floats. Junior and his brother and sisters grudgingly relinquished custody of our floats, and, with chins dragging the surface of the water, also walked the cowards' walk back to the beach. Junior didn't get very far.

"Hey, boy! Gitcher butt awn out here and haul yore momma an' me aroun' some!" Daddy commanded.

"Yo, Junior! Run an' git us a couple o' them cold beers out o' the cooler first," yelled Momma.

"Yes, ma'am," responded poor Junior. "Y'all want Ol' Milwalky or Paps?"

"Jus' brang us a six-pack o' each, boy," Daddy replied. "And hurry up on back ou'cheer so's you can help yore momma up on this dang wobbly thang!"

"Yessir, Daddy."

Junior obediently delivered the brews, and set out helping his very large momma up on her float, while his daddy lay across his, drinking cold beer and watching Junior "tote the weary load."

First, Junior (approximately 13 years old, 5'1" and very sadly overweight) tried lifting his much larger mother under her arms in order to perch her on the float (which seemed to have taken on a life of its own, and actually appeared to be attempting to escape the "Magnitude of Momma"). Well, Momma was apparently extremely ticklish, so Junior's first attempt didn't meet with much success. He then squatted down in the water to hold his cupped hands down for her to step into so that she could board the float "horsey-style." It just so happened that at the very same moment she was throwing her colossal leg over her (a/k/a "my") float, the float moved, sending Momma hiney-first into the water, and causing her to set upon poor Junior like a woman possessed. She whomped the poor boy upside the head, then made him get down an all fours —*underwater*— so she could stand on his back in order to get on the float. And I must say, it appeared that she was taking her dear, sweet time in doing so. A couple of minutes later, poor Junior came up sputtering, gasping, and screaming. Our first thought was that he must have ruptured a disk or something in his valiant, if unsuccessful, effort to make his momma happy. Then we realized why he was screaming in pain. It appeared that something was writhing in his hand, and his hand was rapidly turning blue.

Les and I realized then that a catfish had painfully latched its poisonous barbs into the fleshy inside of Junior's hand.

"Git the sucker out o' my hand! Git the sucker out o' my hand!" ordered the heretofore-timid Junior, at the top of his lungs.

As Les and I ran to his aid, his momma and daddy (still on *our* floats) were yelling excitedly, "JUNOR CAUGHT A FISH! JUNIOR CAUGHT A FISH!"

They were either even more clueless than they looked/acted, or they were just totally oblivious to the pain this young man was obviously feeling — or both.

Les got to him first (good thing), and carefully removed the catfish from Junior's hand, which was already swelling considerably. Les then, without giving the matter a whole lot of thought, sent the catfish flying over a dune in order to prevent further injuries. Momma, panicky after seeing one-sixth (*her* one-sixth, I'm sure) of supper go flying across the sand, yelled, "BUB-ber! Nay-DEEN! Flo-REEN! Y'all git on out o' the water and run git that fish 'fore he dies! Throw 'im in the cooler with y'all's Co-Colers! Don't y'all dare put that nasty, stanky thang in either one of them beer coolers! And y'all git on back out here in the water an' catch me some more fish! If Junior can catch one, I know all y'all can catch some!"

Well, poor things, they tried. Thank heaven they didn't succeed.

Les and I, in the meantime, had gone over to Momma and Daddy to suggest they get Junior to the doctor right away. His hand was still blue and very swollen.

"Oh, he don't need to go to no doctor," offered his daddy. "He's already done had all his school shots."

"Well, actually, I don't think there's a *catfish* shot among those required for admission to school," I disputed, not even attempting to conceal the sarcasm in my voice. "We really do think he should see a doctor. His hand is looking worse and worse by the minute."

"Shucks, this ain't nothin'," countered Momma. "You should'a saw him when he got that whole 'Vyeener' saw-sidge can stuck in his mouth! We pulled an' pulled an' pulled on that dang thang! It

wouldn't budge *none*! Fine'ly, his daddy squirted some WD-40®
'round the edges of the can, and it jes' popped right out! But not
afore Junior laid claim to ever, sangle one o' them 'Vyeener' saw-
sidges — WD-40 an' all! We figured he must'a swallered about a
pint of WD, but it didn't bother him none. And then there was that
time a couple o' years ago — Daddy, you 'member — when he
grabbed that hot dawg from off'n the hy-batchi grill, and it burnt
hy-batchi grill marks in his hands? All we done then was slather
some Parkay® on it, but he kept on lickin' it off before it could do
him any good a'tall. That boy just *loves* Parkay!"

"Momma's right, folks," Daddy said. "Shoot, wunst, he even
had a tar blow right smack up in his face! It was a ol' retread, bald
as a baby's bee-hine. Him and his buddies was drivin' my ol' '63
pickup — he's been drivin' since he was eight — well, they seen
that the right front tar was low, so he took the truck up to the Stop-
N-Shop-R-Swap to put some air in it. Welp, what happened was
he jes' put too much air in that ol' thang and it blowed up on 'im!
KA-BAM! They was little chunks of rubber all over the place!
Hooo whee! Belvin Mathisen, down to the tar store, said he ain't
seen nuthin' like it since he seen a racecar burn slap up. But
Junior wudn't hurt none. The explosion parted his hair in the
middle — permanent, and knocked out all his front teeth, and
cracked four ribs; but other'n 'at, he wudn't hurt none. Nawsir,
Junior's tough. Ain't no liddle ol' catfish gonna git the best o'
him.

"C'mon now, Junior," he continued. "Me and your momma
wants you to pull us out yonder to that buoy 'fore that there barge
comes. We wanna *ride the wake!"*

"Yessir, Daddy."

With that, Les and I decided to pull up stakes and go to any
other spot on the beach. We decided it was worth it to give up our
new floats in order to escape this redneck Twilight Zone. When
we left, we could see the barge coming, and we could hear Junior's
momma and daddy yelling:

"Cain't you go any faster'n 'is, boy? What the heck good are
you doing, anyhow? That barge is gonna be in Noo Ar-leens by
the time we get hife-way acrost this here waterway! And you only
caught *one* fish! What the heck good is *one* fish? That ain't
enough for all of us! Why even bother, if you're just gonna catch
one fish? And he was a little, bitty, puny ol' thang, to boot!"

Feeling sorry for poor Junior, but facing the fact that he was
way beyond our help, Les and I quickly got into our car and

headed much farther down the beach, first stopping to purchase two more floats. We headed east for several miles until we found an isolated spot. We stood atop a sand dune and scanned the horizon in all directions for anything moving and/or breathing, but could see nothing for miles but sand, seagulls, dolphins, and the beautiful Gulf of Mexico. Feeling safe, we unloaded the car, and set about blowing up our new floats. Actually, *I* set about watching *Les* blow up our new floats. We were holding hands and floating lazily with our eyes closed, the delightful Gulf breeze cooling us and taking us slowly back to shore, when suddenly a chill ran down our spines. It was our first reaction to the words:

"*June-yer*! Dawnchew dare drop them dang beer coolers! *Hooo whee*! Yo're right, honeypie! It *is* them same folks from down the way! And look! They got two more bran' new floats! And they're even purdier than the ones they give us! Now you young'uns can play some, too! Only y'all ain't gonna git to ride on that pink shell one! That one's *mine*! An' Daddy gits that chair one! Hey, folks! It's us from the other beach! Hang on! June-yer's comin' out to gitcher floats!"

Les and I decided to paddle out and take our chances with Castro. We had absolutely nothing to lose. With our luck, however, Fidel would be fishing from the end of a dock in Havana, look north, and yell (in Spanish, of course), "*Hooo whee, . . . !*"

SCHOOL DAZE

School starts soon. My eleventh-grader will have to start waking up at the time she's been going to bed all summer. My ninth-grader will have to have the C.D. remote control surgically removed from her hand. And I will once again be asking the same old answerless questions, "What do you mean you don't have anything to wear to school?" and "Didn't I ask you last night to lay out everything you plan to wear today?"

The one I hate most is the first one. We just took out a second mortgage on the house, pawned my jewelry, sold the good china, and rented out the dogs so we could buy our kids' school clothes. (Okay, so I exaggerated a little — we didn't rent out the dogs.) But when kids have to wear clothes with everyone's name on them but their own, it's more than a little frustrating to hear them say, on the first day of school, "Mom! I can*not* go to school today! I don't have *anything* to wear!" Especially when you know their closets are bursting at the seams. Spare me.

"When I was your age," I reminded my firstborn, " I had to . . . ."

"I know, Mom," she continued for me. "You had to walk ten miles each way to school in the sleet and snow in your threadbare gingham dress with the hem hanging out and a rip in the shoulder seam and no socks and your daddy's work boots with newspaper stuffed in the toes so they'd fit, with only a tattered sheet, with a vine for a belt, wrapped around you for warmth, as you carried your turnip green sandwich to school in a pail. Well, Mom, I just want you to know that I talked to Granny, and she told me you lived only two blocks from school, that it never snowed in Mobile back then, that you would only wear the very most expensive and stylish shoes and clothes. So, is there anything else you want to tell me about your deprived childhood?"

"Yeah, well, she's . . . she's delusional — from the poverty."

"Oh, just give it up, Mom. I'm wise to you."

"Well, we didn't have air-conditioning in school," I mumbled.

One thing that has changed, though, is "coverage" (the parts of girls' bodies that must be covered in order for them to be allowed to stay at school). Their shorts and skirts must be no shorter than their fingertips when their arms are at rest by their sides. When I went to school, if a girl's *knees* showed, she was sent home in disgrace. And shorts? The closest we came to shorts in school were the hideous one-piece "gym suits" we had to wear, complete with those sexy "built-in bloomers." It says a whole lot for the boys I went to high school with that they were able to conjure up wolf whistles and other mating calls as the girls ran around the track with those revolting things on. Well, that was the only time they were able to even see our knees, so I guess the reason for their excitement was obvious.

And now we have to have "new makeup" for school.

"Well, you surely don't expect me to go back to school looking like I did *last* year, do you?" I'm asked. "I did the pastel flower-child thing last year. This year, I want to start out smoky and sultry. You know, coal-black mascara and eyeliner, and gunmetal gray eye shadow."

"Smoky and sultry? You're 16 years old!" I reminded her. "You should be going for Dorothy from the 'Wizard of Oz' here — not Lauren Bacall!"

"*Who?*"

"Never mind. The pale makeup is fine. You don't need smoky and sultry. I'm thinking 'smoke-free and cool.' Isn't that a look? You know, brown mascara and light pink eye shadow? Or, better yet, no mascara and no eye shadow. That's a good look. Natural, you know. Boys love that look!"

"Nice try, Mom. Maybe that's okay for you. You're 50. You don't even *have* to look good anymore; you already *have* Daddy. But you just don't understand. It's a very competitive world out there in high school. Some woman is always trying to take your man. That's why I have to look my best. I just want to be able to compete in the marketplace, so to speak. But thanks for the advice. Now, can we please run to the mall and let me pick up just a few more things, Best-Momma-in-the-World?"

"The keys are in the car. Let's get it over with," I relented, walking out the door on the way to the mall — no makeup, gingham dress (with a fan belt tied around the waist) with the hem hanging out, wearing my husband's wading boots with newspaper crammed in the toes.

CLEAR THE ROADS!

M y firstborn baby girl got her learner's permit today — and drove for the first time. I sat in the front seat with her. I aged a great deal. She doesn't like me very much at the moment. Says I'm "paranoid." And "overly critical." I'll let you be the judge.

"Sweetie, I'm very proud of you," I told her as we left the Drivers License Office.

"Thanks, Mom. Can I drive home?"

"Honey, I said that I'm proud of you. I did not say I have a death wish."

"Well, thanks for the vote of confidence. That says a lot about how much you trust me," she said. The June air turned icy.

"It's not *you* I don't trust. It's . . . ."

"I know! I know! It's the *other* drivers," she completed my sentence for me. She does that a lot. The child must be psychic. "I'll watch out for them! I *promise*! Mom, *please* let me drive. I've been waiting for this moment my entire life! I'll be careful. Besides, you'll be right beside me. What can possibly go wrong?"

What, indeed; but the nasal whine of my child won out over prudence.

"Okay, I'll let you drive, but not here. There's too much traffic."

"Sure, no problem."

She had won. She could afford to be magnanimous.

Ten miles up the highway, I pulled onto a side road and let her take the wheel. It was a four-lane highway with little traffic so early in the afternoon.

She turned back onto the highway. The speed limit was 65.

"Honey, you're only going 20 miles per hour. You might want to speed up."

I should've been more specific. She gunned it. We were going 80.

"*Not this fast!*" I shrieked.

"Well, you don't have to *yell* at me," she said, her bottom lip protruding all the way to the steering wheel.

"I'm sorry, sweetie. Just slow down, please."

She slammed on the brakes. We were going 20 again. I discovered that the passenger-side seat belt worked.

"You don't have to hit the brakes so hard. Just let off on the accelerator. You'll slow down fast enough."

— 69 —

"Okay. Sorry," she replied.

"You might want to stay between the lines in the middle and the solid one on the right," I suggested.

"I'm trying. This car is just too wide. I really think it's, like, wider than the lanes are," she informed me. "Don't you think we should rent a smaller car for a couple of weeks? Just 'til I kinda get the feel of driving?"

"Or maybe you'd rather just drive '*Big Momma*'," I threatened. "Big Momma" is my husband's aged, oversized tank of a minivan with more than a quarter of a million miles on it.

"No, *please*! Not *that* thing! If I were seen driving that old clunker, I'd never be able to face anybody again! We'd have to move to another *country*! Please, Mom, not that!"

The threat worked.

"Okay. You're doing fine. Just stay at this speed, and watch your lines on both sides," I cautioned her.

"*OOOH! OOOH!*" she screamed.

"*What! What is it?*" I yelled, as I grabbed the dashboard and applied the imaginary brakes on my side of the floorboard.

"I *love* this song! And I *never* get to hear it!" she explained, reaching for the volume control on the radio, while veering into the grass on the right side of the road.

"*Carly!*" I screeched, "*Watch where you're going!*"

"O-*kay*! O-*kay*! You don't have to *yell* at me," she whimpered.

"I'm sorry, honey. Just don't fool with the radio when you're driving. You need to really concentrate on driving. Let's just turn this thing off for a while."

I turned off the radio. The silence was deafening. And there was that chill again.

"I can't drive with the radio off," she huffily informed me.

"Fine. I can. Just pull over."

"*No*! I'll just try harder," she relented.

After twenty miles or so, I suggested that she make a U-turn in a paved area in the median.

"Just make sure no one's coming up behind you, turn on your left blinker, and get into the left lane."

She looked in the rearview and sideview mirrors. Water suddenly sprayed the windshield, and the wipers started sweeping furiously.

"*What's happening?*" she cried.

"You just turned on the windshield washer instead of the turn signal. No big deal. Just turn them off and turn your blinker on."

That worked. We were now heading south, also known as "home." She was driving 20 miles per hour again.

"Honey, speed up — *just a little at a time*, though."

A short while later, we approached an 18-wheeler carrying a load of molten sulfur. It was in the right-hand lane, as we were, and was moving very slowly, as we *weren't*.

"You might want to slow down, sugar," I advised her.

She lifted her foot off the accelerator.

"*Now!*" I screamed.

She hit the brake — 65 to 20 — in a second-and-a half. Seat belt still works.

"You *don't* have to *yell*," she reminded me indignantly. "How do you expect me to *ever* learn to drive if you keep *yelling* at me all the time?"

"I *had* to yell! We were about to plow right into the back of that truck! You have to learn to slow down when you come up behind someone that quickly."

"Well, I wish you'd make up your mind! You just told me ten minutes ago *not* to slam on the brakes!" she argued. "You said to just take my foot off the accelerator."

"When I told you that, there wasn't a huge truck with hot stinky stuff in it three car lengths ahead of us!"

"*Three?* You *always* exaggerate when you get mad! That truck was, like, *five* lengths ahead of us!" she fired back.

"Okay. Well, let's just concentrate on getting around it for now."

"*Around* it? You want me to drive *around* this truck? Mom, you've lost it!"

"No, I haven't. You can do this. Just concentrate. Just do what you did when you were getting ready to make the U-turn. Check for other traffic, and turn on your windshield wipers."

"Very funny."

She doesn't appreciate my sense of humor.

She did all that was required of her. She pulled around the truck. As she pulled up alongside it, she looked at me and smiled.

"Well, Mrs. Critical, how was that?"

"That was very good," I commended her.

Then she pulled back over into the right lane.

"*Carly! Not yet!*"

My life flashed before me. (That really does happen, you know.) I snapped my head around and looked behind me. The truck's headlights were in our backseat, and they weren't even turned on.

"*What? What did I do now?*" she wailed.

"You're supposed to wait until you completely *pass* the truck before you pull back over into the right lane!"

"Well, you don't have to *yell* at me! I can't concentrate if you keep yelling like that!"

"It comes with the territory, honey. You'll just have to get used to it," I told her as my heart slid slowly back down into my chest.

With the truck safely behind us, the remainder of the ride home was relatively unremarkable — if you don't count the wide turns, the stopping for green lights, and the hydrangeas she "pruned" with the right fender.

Her dad was waiting for us as she pulled into the driveway.

"How'd it go?" he asked.

"It was great except your paranoid wife kept *yelling* at every little thing I did. You'd have thought I spent the whole time running into things," Carly informed him.

He looked at me. I shrugged.

"Was it really that bad?" he asked.

"Nah. I guess I just overreacted," I told him as I pulled hydrangea branches off the fender.

"You do tend to do that, you know," he informed me. "You really just need to relax and not get so anxious."

"Daddy!" Carly said, "My sweet, sweet Daddy. Will you let me drive to the mall, *please*?"

"Sure, honey. Got your permit with you?"

"Right here in my purse," she told him. "Daddy, do you mind if we take Mom's car?"

"That's fine. It might be easier for you to drive," he responded.

They kissed me goodbye and hopped into my car. I watched them head down the street. And I listened.

"*Carly! Watch out for that mailbox!*"

"Well, *good grief*, Daddy! You don't have to *yell* at me!"

And I grinned.

HUMILIATION BY PARENT

H as anything yet taken the place of cod liver oil (interchangeable with castor oil) as both a miracle cure for any disease
and the best incentive in the world to make a wayward child
"straighten up and fly right?"

I remember Poor Ol' Johnny Paul Cooper (that's what everybody called him). When we were kids, his mother would chase
him down — *outside*, in full view of all of his friends — and get
his twin little brothers to sit on his arms while she pinched his nose
to cut off his breathing so he'd have to open his mouth to get air.
That's when she'd use this huge, horse medicine dropper (at least,
that's what it *looked* like) to drizzle about a half-gallon of that
slimy, stinky stuff into his open, howling mouth. And all the
while, she's yelling (loud enough for every single kid in the entire
neighborhood to hear), "Now, John, you might just as well stay
still and swallow this medicine! You'll thank me for it when you
get *regular!*"

Those of us who were his friends could commiserate with Poor
Ol' Johnny Paul Cooper, and we could certainly suffer his
humiliation along with him. We had all been there before; well,
not necessarily "there," but we were all subject to (and much more
often than not, the ill-fated recipients of): *Mortification at the
Hands of Our Parents.*

It came in so many forms. Of course, Poor Ol' Johnny Paul
Cooper was definitely a worst-case scenario. My mom never did
the cod liver oil thing to me; she couldn't catch me. But never at
any time that she heard his mom imposing regularity-by-fish-
lubricant upon Poor Ol' Johnny Paul Cooper did she fail to ask,
"Now, aren't you glad Mommy makes you eat your turnip greens
and collards?" I remember wondering (to myself, of course),
"Why this irrational compulsion on the part of mothers to restore
bowel regularity to their kids?" (Although those probably weren't
the *exact* words I used at ten years of age.)

But the absolute worst — and most emotionally scarring —
humiliation parents can *ever* inflict upon their kids is to *dance* in
front of their kids' friends. The first time I saw that happen was at
a school dance when I was in the tenth grade. Donna Pearson's
mom and dad were two of the parent chaperones. There were
several other parents there, but they didn't do anything to really
embarrass their kids. They all either jitterbugged or slow-danced

(with actual space between their bodies) — "old people" dances. But not the Pearsons! They *twisted*! Never mind that *nobody* twisted anymore! Never mind that they were the absolute *worst* twisters in the entire *world*! Never mind that Mrs. Pearson twisted with her head all the way back the whole time, with her eyes squeezed shut and her mouth wide open like she was *gargling* or something; or that Mr. Pearson fell flat on his tail every time he squatted down to do a low twist, and several of the boys had to go over and pull him back up on his feet each time.

As if that weren't bad enough, the Pearsons insisted on hauling loudly protesting students out on the gym floor all night long to twist with them. *Poor Donna.* She stayed in the girls' restroom all night, crying and bemoaning her misfortune at having been cursed with this particular set of parents. The rest of us girls tried to comfort her by assuring her that, at some point in time, this had either happened to us, or would in the foreseeable future; although we (and she) all knew that nothing and *no one* could ever top her parents on the Mortification Scale. Consequently, nothing we said offered her much comfort.

The Pearsons chaperoned every dance we ever had in high school, and they *twisted* at all of them.

Donna moved, all by herself, to Iceland the summer after we graduated from high school. She left no forwarding address. Rumor has it there's a whole commune of "Adult Children of Chaperones" there, and all of its members have wisely chosen to remain childless.

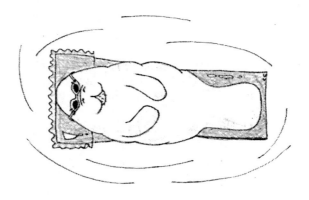

THE 6,912,874-SECOND SUMMER

A s I type this, there are six days, fourteen hours, seventeen minutes and eleven seconds until school starts; but who's counting? Please don't interpret my knowing just how long I have 'til "Independence Day" to mean that I haven't enjoyed every single second I've spent with my 13- and 15-year-old daughters this summer (all 6,912,874 of them). And I'll miss them terribly while they're in school; but I'll be happy to retire all the vast and sundry hats I've had to wear all summer: Recreation Director, Mediator, Psychologist, Referee, Chef, Short-Order Cook, Chauffeur, Laundress, Seamstress, Suntan Lotion Slatherer, Personal Shopper, Maid, and, most importantly, Loan Officer a/k/a "Patsy."

School may have been out, but *I* certainly learned a great deal this summer, including, but most assuredly *not limited to*, the following:

Seventy-eight television channels are not nearly enough. If they were, then I wouldn't have to hear, fifty times a day, "There's *nothing* on TV!" (There were three channels when I was their ages.)

Children my kids' ages do not "go outside and get some fresh air." They'd sweat, spontaneously combust, or something equally as unpleasant.

Mornings that start before 1:00 P.M. result in *very* crabby children because the TV that has "nothing on" it *never* goes off the air.

And because we live a half-hour from the Gulf of Mexico, my daughters (now, apparently, the world's youngest marine biologists), after having been stung several times, have concluded: Jellyfish serve no useful purpose.

My two teenagers can consume enough food in ten weeks of summer vacation to feed the entire Russian Army for twelve years. (Does Russia still have an army?)

Their friends, who have apparently established summer residence at our house, can consume even more.

Jellyfish serve no useful purpose.

I am the only non-working mother in my children's groups of friends; and it is, indeed, *quite* possible to put 176,000 miles on one's car in ten weeks.

Sunblock is for nerds. (*Their* conclusion; not mine.)

Teenagers really don't care that money doesn't grow on trees.

There actually *is* such a thing as spending too much time at the mall.

A mother's presence is not required at the mall (only her money).

Jellyfish serve no useful purpose.

And last, but certainly not least, water parks do *not* cater to adults. (Therefore, if an adult gets totally stuck in an innertube while floating [and I use the term loosely] down an overcrowded, winding, aqua-colored, fake river with turbulent currents, and with only her arms and legs and the very top of her head sticking out of the tube hole while she's flailing and thrashing and screaming for help, and making a complete fool of herself, she's *pretty much on her own.*)

JUST LOOK WHAT JULIUS CAESAR'S MOMMA STARTED

I'll never forget the day, several years ago, when I took my two young daughters with me to "that" toy store to buy a birthday gift for my nephew. I made the mistake of taking a shortcut down the dreaded "Barbie® aisle."

"Ooh! Mommy! Mommy! A bran'-new *BARBIE!*" screamed my four-year-old daughter. "I don't even *have* her yet!"

"Carly, darling, she looks just like all your other Barbies. She just has different clothes," I told her.

"She does not *either* look like all my other Barbies!" Carly argued. "Her hair is differenter."

"Her hair is long and blonde," I reasoned. "What is different about *this* particular Barbie's hair?"

"It's more *wavier.*"

"Wavier?" I questioned, still unable to detect even a subtle difference.

"Yes, ma'am. It's *lots* more wavier — and her eyelashers are lots more longer," she countered.

"Well, honey, that may very well be, but you already have seven Barbies. You don't need another. Besides, we're here to shop for your cousin, not for you or your sister."

"That's not *fair*, Mommy! You always do stuff for other people's little kids. You never do *anything* for *me!*" wailed the poor, pitiful, little waif whose toy collection has outgrown her toy box, her closet, her room, and now needs a house of its own.

"I never do anything for you? Well, what about those nine months that I carried you around in my tummy? And I gave birth to you, too. Did you forget about that?"

"I didn't forget. But Jennifer's mommy said that I was born from a 'Sarium' section and that that doesn't even count. She said it only counts if you have to scream for five days and say lots of dirty words and call your husband mean things," she informed me.

"Oh, she did, did she?" I said to myself. "Doesn't count, eh? Oh, if she only knew."

I remember my first reaction, all those years ago, when I first learned from my obstetrician that I would need to deliver Carly via Caesarean (or "Sarium") section: "Yea! No labor pains!"

I had heard all the war stories from my women friends about their two weeks of labor, their 60-inch episiotomies, their addiction to hemorrhoid medication, and on and on, ad nauseam. My low pain threshold and I were not looking forward to any of that. Consequently, I celebrated (inwardly) when my doctor told me that chances were extremely slim that I would experience any of the discomfort that goes along with a "normal" delivery.

What he forgot to tell me was what I *would* experience — in particular, what I'd experience *post*-delivery.

First of all, immediately after Carly's birth I had a nurse assigned to me who made Nurse Ratched on "One Flew Over the Cuckoo's Nest" look like Marmee on "Little Women." She had me up and out of bed the first thing the morning after *major* surgery, regardless of the fact that I had 14,897 (well, it *felt* like 14, 897) *staples* in my lower abdomen. It was then that The Wicked Nurse of the South informed me that *we* were "going for a little walk." In the first place, I didn't *want* to go for a walk — little or any other kind. I wanted to do only two things: hold my baby and sleep — in *that* order. I quickly learned that in the maternity ward, as in the real world, it did not matter in the least what *I* wanted. The only consolation Nurse Wretched could give me was that I would not be alone on my coerced excursion. She had dragged yet another of "my kind" into the hallway to wobble along with me.

She dragged me (along with the bed, IV pole, and nightstand I so desperately clung to in a futile effort to avoid being compelled to leave the relative safety of my room) into the hall where I joined my gloomy-faced fellow hunchback. There, Nurse "Wretched" did what amounted to lining the two of us up at the proverbial "starting gate." So, there we were, hooked up to our IV poles, slumped over like 110-year-old women, holding our 40-pound, stapled bellies in the hope that nothing would fall out, and she (the aforementioned nursewitch) is yelling, "Head 'em up! Moo-o-o-o-o-o-ve 'em out!" The spectators (among whom were other nurses and "Express Delivery" moms who had delivered the hour before and were standing in the hall, eating their "Bonus Burgers") found this absolutely *hilarious*; we (the hunchbacks) failed to find any humor *whatsoever* in it.

In many maternity wards, this little humiliation parade that post-Caesarean moms are heartlessly forced to take is called "The Caesarean Shuffle." Those of us who have participated in it find the term "Death March" more suitable. It consisted, basically, of a round trip of the one-floor maternity ward. Sounds like no big deal, right? Wrong. It's a *very* big deal when the walkers are unable to lift their slippered feet from the floor (hence, the term "shuffle"); remove their hands from their substantial, stapled bellies; walk without leaning on their unstable IV poles for support; or moo-oo-oo-oo-oove more than twenty steps without begging to lie down.

The memory of this experience was still all too vivid to me as Carly (the "deliver*ee*") accused me of "not doing anything" for her. Realizing that the details were a little too graphic to share with a four-year-old, I consoled myself with the knowledge that in another 25 or 30 years, she too would be strolling down a toy store aisle, the victim of the same allegations.

I could wait.

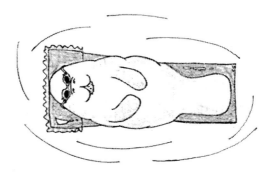

THE MAYBERRY ZONE

O ne of the most frightening, recurring nightmares I have is where I'm 30 years old, single, and living in Mayberry, North Carolina around the mid-1960s. As if that weren't bad enough, there's this invisible force field (sort of like in "Lost in Space") surrounding the entire area, so escape is totally out of the question. The nightmare is actually a terrifying mixture of "The Andy Griffith Show" and "The Twilight Zone," sort of *"The Mayberry Zone."*

Not wanting to *never* date again, but realizing my limitations (man-wise) in this little town, I take an inventory of its eligible (for lack of a better word) bachelors. That's what makes it a true nightmare rather than simply a dream, or even a really, really *bad* dream.

Here's the roster (in order from "Least Repugnant" to "Being a Spinster is Definitely *Not* the Worst Thing in the World"):

BACHELOR NUMBER ONE: ANDY TAYLOR

Andy is the "High Sheriff" (or "Shurf") of Mayberry. He has a respectable, if somewhat low-end, job. His future is in the hands of the voters; but since there's absolutely no one else in town who is nearly as capable of handling the "shurfin'" duties, his job is relatively secure. Unfortunately, Andy is just as happy as a mule eatin' briars being the Sheriff of Mayberry, North Carolina; and, as a result, has zero aspirations to move onward and upward (definitely *not* a good thing).

As Sheriff of a very small town, his salary is negligible; but he has a nice, comfortable house and a spinster aunt who could do all the cooking and cleaning, so I wouldn't have to. Now there's a *big* point in Andy's favor. He also has a son who's a pretty neat little kid. I am a bit concerned, however, with the fact that Andy named him "Opie." I mean, what if Andy and I did get married and have children? Would he insist on naming them something like "Scoopie" or "Floppie"; or, heaven forbid, would he want to stay in that same Opie "sphere" and name them "Mopie" or "Nopie" or

"Dopie?" That's a substantial, undeniable concern to me when it comes to looking at High Sheriff Andy Taylor as a potential date. Add to that his fondness for "settin' on the front porch" strumming his guitar and singing nothing but bluegrass music, and I'm thinking, "Let's just take a *little* look-see at who else is available."

BACHELOR NUMBER TWO: BARNEY FIFE

Deputy Sheriff Barney Fife is Andy's right-hand "man" (and I use the term *very* loosely). While there is a pretty good bit of job security for "Barn" (as Andy calls him), his salary is virtually non-existent. He lives in a sparsely-furnished room on the top floor of a widow lady's boarding house. His décor consists of a high-school pennant hanging above his single bed. He has a solitary bare light bulb hanging from the ceiling. Unbeknownst to his landlady, he also has a hotplate in there. She'd evict him if she ever found out. He knows the rules, yet he has the courage to mock them. He's a bit of a rebel. I *like* that in a man.

Barney's knowledge of fashion is as infinitesimal as his salary. He has one suit (tweed), complete with bow tie (deduct several points for this one) and two "grandpa" hats (sort of silly, Fedora things — one for winter and a lighter version for summer). Barn's quite the fashion plate. As Deputy Sheriff, he does, of course, wear a uniform to work. However, there are some men even a uniform can't help. His physique also leaves a bit to be desired — actually, it leaves an *enormous* amount to be desired. The words "diminutive" and even "petite" could unquestionably be used to describe Barney. He weighs maybe 105 pounds, dripping wet, with his clothes on, and his holster and gun, . . . and his hand-cuffs, . . . and his bullet, . . . *and* some horseshoes; has an 18" waistline; and appears to be suffering from osteoporosis in his 30's. He has no chest or hiney, and there is nothing even *remotely* resembling a muscle or even a tendon in his entire body.

Let's move on. *Please.*

BACHELOR NUMBER THREE: GOMER PYLE

I've heard it said by certain prominent Mayberry residents (who should certainly know) that Gomer is the result of marital relations between his momma and daddy. While that, in and of itself, isn't the least bit unusual, when the further speculation is made that his momma and daddy were *first cousins*, well . . . . And if you spend any time with Gomer, you realize that this is not at all an unlikely story. While the essence of generosity and gentle spirit, Gomer, to put it nicely, ain't too bright. His primary polysyllabic words are "sha-*zye-um*," "gaaawwwaaaaawwaaaww-*lee*," and "suh-*praz,* suh-*praz*, suh-*praz*!" He works down at Wally's Service Station, but he's not good at much when it comes to cars except for putting in gasoline and washing windshields. Wally's shown him about 30 times where the radiator is in a car, but poor Gomer keeps "disremembering." But he's *such* a nice guy — ugly as sin, but nice -- *really, really* nice. He has the intelligence of a doorknob; but he's *so* nice. And he put the "g" in goofy; still he's *awfully* nice. But since any date is a potential father for a woman's children, we'd best move along — *now*!

BACHELOR NUMBER FOUR: FLOYD, THE BARBER

Floyd is a quaint, little fellow. "Meek" would also describe him well. Once, he almost shouted. Nearly scared the little pants off Barney. Of all the bachelors in Mayberry, Floyd is probably the best-off, financially; although that's not saying much. He owns a barber shop, apparently the only one in town; and thus has unlimited job security, particularly in light of the fact that it looks like all the men in town get their hair cut every other day. Of course, if he and I were to "get serious," I'd have to *insist* that he raise the price of his haircuts from $1.00. There's just no way in the world we could retire in Florida on that kind of money.

And Floyd *does* have a tendency to . . . mumble, so . . . .

BACHELOR NUMBER FIVE: ERNEST T. BASS

If poor Gomer was the result of the marital relations between *first cousins*, then Ernest T.'s momma and daddy had to be *brother and sister*. This is a truly bizarre, eccentric, alien man. He skips, bounces, shrieks, throws rocks, giggles, howls, and scares the good citizens of Mayberry half to death. Granted, once he gets cleaned up, he's a lot easier to look at than Barney and Gomer (like that's saying a whole lot); but the man is a certifiable *lunatic*. He's deranged. He's possessed. He's a frightening, little (to use his own word) "creach-ter." But invariably, in my nightmare, *he's* the one standing beside me at the altar.

Fortunately, I always awaken (usually screaming) just as the Justice of the Peace (also the role of Sheriff Taylor) asks, "Will you, Rebel, take Ernest T. to be your 'awfully-wedded' . . . *creach-ter*?"

It's no wonder "Ain't" Bea never got married.

SAMANTHA STEVENS:
ONE DUMB WITCH

My ultimate fantasy is to be Samantha from "Bewitched," or, better yet, Jeannie from "I Dream of Jeannie." Jeannie had better hair, a better body, cooler clothes, was more fun, and was nowhere *near* as hung up on housework as Samantha was. Granted, Samantha was much more realistic, and probably — no, *undoubtedly* — a much better "traditional" wife. She fit the mold, so to speak. And while I really liked Samantha, I can't help but think she was just entirely too submissive. Even when Darrin was at work, and had *no* earthly idea what she was doing at home, she'd still wash dishes by hand, cook the conventional way, vacuum, dust, wash baseboards, mop, and actually sort laundry, which she would later wash, dry, fold, iron, hang, and put away.

Silly woman.

I just can't understand it. I mean, why do all that drudge work *voluntarily* (and actually *enjoy* doing it)? Why not just cross her arms, and nod, blink, and twitch it into being? Personally, *that* (crossing, nodding, blinking, and twitching) is *my* version of the ideal way to get dinner on the table.

While Samantha was pouring, mixing, and shaking Darrin's martinis, Jeannie was simply *nodding* Tony's into existence. While Samantha was slaving over a hot stove and oven, making pot roast, mashed potatoes, corn, broccoli, and yeast rolls, Jeannie was simply blinking up Caesar salad, filet mignon, sautéed mushrooms, artichoke hearts, hollandaise sauce, and cherries jubilee. While Samantha was sweeping, polishing, and scrubbing toilets and bathtubs, Jeannie and Tony were doing the "Funky Chicken" at the Whiskey-A-Go-Go. And while Samantha was agonizing over which polyester, double-knit, daisy-encrusted orange outfit she should wear to yet another of Darrin's dull office functions, Jeannie had already blinked up the funky, white vinyl, belly-button-revealing mini-skirt with matching crop top, billed vinyl cap, and white, knee-high go-go boots for her evening out with Tony at the Officers' Club.

Samantha, on the other hand, was as close to being June Cleaver as a person with "powers" can be. But she was a *witch*, for Pete's sake. Society tends to frown upon such. Jeannie, on the other hand, was a "genie." And if a guy brings home to momma two such women as prospective brides, which is momma gonna like better? Is it gonna be the witch or the genie? Well, I know for one thing that if some boy's momma in Kushla, Alabama is given that choice, it sure as heck ain't gonna be a *witch*!

Besides, I could never understand what the big deal was with Darrin Stevens. Why did he have such a hang-up about Samantha just "twitching up" a meal? Or cleaning up the house "via twitch?" Fuddy Duddy.

I must admit, however, despite my personal preference for Jeannie's "style," I still have quite a bit of trouble with that "Master" stuff. Thankfully, she did finally get around to calling him "Tony."

My husband has expressed, on many occasions while we're watching "I Dream of Jeannie" reruns, that he wouldn't be at all opposed to my wearing little genie outfits while I twitch him up some martinis and call him "Master." Every time he feels the need to share that little fantasy with me, I take the opportunity to thump him upside the head.

Sometimes, thumps are even more powerful than twitches — at least around our house.

THE CROCODILE HUNTER
HAS NOTHING ON ME

TV's newest hero appears to be an Australian fellow with a death wish. His name is Steve Irwin, but he is known as "The Crocodile Hunter." Steve has what amounts to nearly a "cult" following. My husband, kids, and I watch him every chance we get. He's either the bravest man on Earth or the dumbest — or *both*. He "plys" with "snikes," and considers Komodo dragons and the like "gorgeous." He picks up angry rattlesnakes (or "snikes"), and he wrestles with thousand-pound crocodiles. He lets tarantulas crawl on his "fice" (the part of his body that contains — at least *so far* — his eyes, nose and mouth). The guy is certifiable. I guess the attraction is that most of us who watch him would never, in a million or so years, ever place ourselves in the kind of danger Steve does. Yet I wonder how brave Steve really is. I wonder if he has the courage, the backbone, and the nerves of steel it takes to do what I do daily. No, I'm not talking about looking at myself in the mirror with *bedhair* and last night's makeup still on. I'm talking about actually going into that most frightening of all places on Earth — *the teenager's bedroom*. That trek would turn even Steve Irwin's hair white. I should know. I've been there — and lived to tell about it.

It was *horrible* — twenty-three empty Coke® cans with ABC (already-been-chewed) gum stuck to the tops, remnants of what appeared to be either chicken bones or petrified waffles, cotton balls or cotton candy (inedible, regardless of what they were), a stuffed kangaroo with a Barbie® head in its pouch; a plastic shark with a Barney® body stuck in its mouth; 4,782 bottles of nail polish; and a floor composed entirely of clothes and shoes. I distinctly remember having carpeting installed in there when we built the house. She walked in as I was surveying the whole scene.

"Hi, Mom. 'Sup?" she queried, innocently.

"What's *up*?" I responded, unbelievably. "What's *up*? That's what *I'd* like to know! What happened *in here*?"

"What do you mean?"

"What do you *mean*, what do I mean?"

"I mean, what are you talking about?" she asked.

"I'm talking about this room. Is there still a floor under there?"

"Well, duh, Mom. Are you trying to insinuate something?"

"Nope. I'm not *insinuating* anything. This room is *hideous*!"

"I know," she responded. "It really is. So, when am I getting new furniture and getting it painted?"

"Surely you jest," I laughed. "The walls are covered with peanut butter and *something*, and the furniture is hidden under clothes and cans and penicillin bread. You can't *seriously* think that Daddy and I are going to redecorate it for you."

"Oh, good grief! *Of course not!* You and Daddy have absolutely *no* idea what I even want in here," she informed me. "I'm thinking we get rid of this bed and get a daybed and some white rattan furniture. We paint the walls cobalt blue and get a white down comforter and lots of really pretty throw pillows for my bed. Then, we . . . ."

"You're missing my point entirely, darling," I told her. "My point *is* that there will be no redecorating; and nothing new will go in here until you learn to keep your room clean."

"Oh, you're talking about the fact that it's a teeny bit messed up, aren't you? Well, it won't take me 15 minutes to straighten this up. Then can we go and look for new furniture and bedding?"

"No, we cannot. But you *will* clean this room before you talk on the phone again. Got it?"

"I don't know why you're getting so upset. It's not that bad. You should see *Kelly's* room, if you think *mine* is bad."

I didn't even want to *think* about Kelly's room if it was worse than this. I guess that's why Kelly's parents stopped entertaining when she turned 13.

"I told you not to get on that phone 'til your room is clean," I reminded her fifteen minutes later when she emerged from her room, phone attached to ear.

"It's clean."

I walked past her to inspect her work product, fear and dread (and the normal state of her room) causing me to tremble slightly. What had happened? It was just this side of an actual miracle. The bed was made. The carpet had grown back. There were no cola cans stuck to the wall. No JELL-O® bones. Even the previously-chewed, rigidified gum had been expunged from all the windowpanes. How could she have done that so quickly? I was torn between surprise and total disbelief. And then, . . . I very cautiously opened her closet door. Twelve tons of clothes, belts, shoes, purses, posters, books, photo albums, cola cans, waffle-fossils, and a really scary Barney head attached to the body of Barbie burst through the doors and knocked me to the ground.

Crocodiles, rattlesnakes, tarantulas? *Please.*

BUBBAHOOD

W e Southerners (a whole bunch of us, anyway) seem to have a fondness for nicknames, more so probably than folks from other parts of the country. I know, of course, that nicknames are, by no means, limited to the South. For instance, there's "Rocky," a primarily New York-type nickname. I've met three "Slims" from Oklahoma; eighty-six "Sandys/Sandis/Sandees" from California; a "Muffy," a "Midge," and a "Minksy" from New England; two "Dutches" from up around the Great Lakes; and even one "Ratso" from Chicago. And I would imagine there are any given number of people down here with those nicknames, particularly "Slim." But one would be pretty hard-pressed to find folks living north of the Mason-Dixon Line nicknaming their children (or grandchildren, or anyone they cared *even the slightest for*) "Cooter," "Tooter," "Pooter," or "Skeeter." Then there's "Punkin'" and "Tater" (or his saccharine sister "Sweet Tater") and "Sugar Boy" and "Ladybug."

The one I personally find the most disgusting, embarrassing (for the entire region), and hardest to understand is the infamous "Booger." Being named after a type of physique ("Slim"), a vegetable ("Tater" and/or "Sweet Tater"), or even an insect ("Skeeter") is one thing; being named after nasal mucous discharge is quite another. There are even infinite variations of "Booger." I've met "Booger Bob," "Booger Ike," "Boogerette," "Boogerella," and even "Sugar Booger" (named, in part, after her daddy, "Sugar Boy"). Then there's "Boogerman" and his first-born son, "Boogerboy," previously known as "Booger*baby*" (what a proud daddy that "Boogerman" must have been). And there's also "Boogerbear" and "Boogerbrain" (what charming images that one brings to mind), and at least four dozen "Booger Reds" — in Mobile, Alabama alone.

But even "Booger" falls short, in sheer numbers, to "Bubba." "Bubba" is, without a doubt, the single most popular nickname bestowed upon *anyone* in the South. It's believed to have first been used back in post-Civil War Chunchula, Alabama by little Dewey

Capps. Little Dewey, it seems, was calling his older brother, Zebedee, which he couldn't even *begin* to pronounce, so he called him — or *tried* to call him — "Brother," only it came out of little Dewey's two-year-old mouth as "Bubba." And this familiar, familial term has been used ever since by many younger siblings to address or refer to an older brother — or even to someone who's no kin to anybody, I suppose.

While not wanting to offend any of the "Boogers" of the South, I have to admit I'm a lot more comfortable with "Bubba" than I am with "Booger." It (the nickname "Bubba") is as much a part of life in the South as watermelon, pickled pigs' feet, or Southeastern Conference football.

I've known a "Bubba" with a Ph.D., a "Bubba" who's a dentist; an Episcopalian priest, Father "Bubba" (although his congregation doesn't refer to him that way); and even an interior decorator named "Bubba." I've also known "Bubbas" who are generals, airline pilots, and singers in rock bands.

Back (*way* back) in college, some of my women friends and I had such a fondness for the name that we even formed a "Bubba-hood of Sisters." We spoke "Bubbaspeak," i.e., we substituted the name/word "Bubba" for the word "brother" every time we spoke or read the latter. For instance, there was that very soulful '60s duo, "The Righteous *Bubbas*," and, of course, the pioneers of flight, Orville and Wilbur, the Wright *Bubbas*. Your sister was married, of course, to your "*bubba*-in-law." Our favorite song was the haunting "He Ain't Heavy, He's My *Bubba*." Our dream for the world (and the dream of all Miss Universe contestants) was that all of its inhabitants could live in peace and *bubbaly* love.

Most of the Bubbas I've known have even *looked* like they *could* and/or *should* be called "Bubba." Unlike "Timmy" or "Mikey" or "Petey," the name "Bubba" isn't easily outgrown. I'd be willing to bet that Bill Clinton still answers to it when he goes back to Hope, Arkansas. I can easily picture a young James Earl "Bubba" Carter, and maybe even Lyndon Baines "Bubba" Johnson. What's hard for me to imagine, however, is a 30-ish Rose Kennedy standing on the porch of the main house of the Hyannis Port compound, yelling out in the darkness to John, "Bubba, you git your butt on in here for dinner!"

(Besides, you don't call a *real* Bubba to dinner after dark. That, of course, would be *supper*. Even a moron knows that dinner's *'round noon* down here!)

HUNTIN' OR HONEYMOONIN'
— MAKE UP YOUR MIND

A s a person who still sobs every time she watches "Bambi," and hears that fateful shot that killed his momma, I never have quite fit in with the rest of my paternal extended family.

I'm still harboring a tremendous amount of guilt because thirty-something years ago at my grandmother's house, I made the mistake of calling my family to the window to see the cute little bunny that was munching down in my grandmother's garden. The next thing I knew, my stepfather disappeared, there was a loud "BLAM" sound outside, and we were eating mystery meat and rice for dinner. My stepfather said it was chicken. Yeah, "Thumper" the chicken.

All of my male cousins on my stepdaddy's side teethed on shotgun shells, and had to be able to fire a big, ol' 12-gauge shotgun without being knocked down by it before their first pimple appeared. If not, they were called "Susie" for a year.

These male cousins and their daddies also fish. But they don't "deep sea" fish. ("That's for them doctor and lawyer yuppie types. That's dadgum sissy fishin!") These aforementioned cousins and uncles are mostly "bice" (a/k/a bass) fishermen. They like those "wad-mouth" (a/k/a wide-mouthed) bice. They, being of the large-mouthed species themselves, can certainly relate to that particular fish.

Huntin' and fishin' (singular) is their life (also singular). My cousin Barry's wife, Dianne, made the mistake of marrying him right smack-dab in the middle of deer season. As a result, she spent her honeymoon at the less-than-luxurious family hunting camp in Pennington, Alabama, the decor of which consists primarily of more than 50 glass-eyed deer heads, complemented stylishly by over 100 sets of detached deer horns and one particularly repulsive set of wild boar tusks, with the head attached.

Fortunately, there was an Alabama football game on TV that weekend; and, since the hunting camp didn't have electricity, and since no self-respecting 'Bama fan is gonna miss a televised game — huntin' season or not, she and Barry got to share the camp with only two uncles and three cousins who are Auburn fans (the "lunatic fringe," as the 'Bama kin prefer to call them). Not only that, but those same uncles and cousins were uncharacteristically gracious enough to let the honeymooners have the only bedroom, but only because Auburn beat Alabama the year before, so they were still in a pretty benevolent mood.

Barry and Dianne have been married for more than 20 years, and have never spent an anniversary together. As I said, it's right in the middle of hunting season.

And poor Dianne. She had the misfortune of having been born on the first day of dove season. Consequently, she's received a belated birthday card and plucked doves ready for cooking every year since she's been married to Barry.

As if that weren't bad enough, their only child, a girl (a/k/a "not a hunter"), had the misfortune to be born on the opening day of deer season, so Barry couldn't possibly have been there for "the birthing." But he's been there for two of her sixteen birthdays. He defensively asserted, after having missed her Sweet Sixteen party, "Like it was *my* fault she was born when she was?" Besides, she has all those gun racks her daddy's made for her every year from upturned deer hooves.

But then *I* was the one who committed the ultimate family "atrocity." After having dated a number of hunters/fishermen with whom the male members of my family were delighted and immediately bonded, I found a man who had no idea *whatsoever* when deer or dove season started, and had never even attempted to catch a "wad-mouth bice."

Well, as soon as he politely declined my cousins' invitation to join them for the day for which they all lived — the opening day of deer season, they all rushed to ask me, "What is he — a dadgum *Democrat* or something?"

The fact is that he just doesn't get into shooting birds or doe-eyed animals. And he'd much rather water-ski than fish, although he truly enjoys deep-sea fishing. ("I already *told* you! *That* don't count," argues my Uncle Bud. "It ain't really fishin'!") Yeah, Uncle Bud; we all know it's much easier to catch a 400-pound hammerhead shark than it is to catch a three-pound "wad-mouth bice." That takes a *real* man. Just don't you ever again make the mistake of lumping my man in with *lawyers*! He can bait his *own* hook!

LAP DAWGS, HUNTIN' DAWGS, PORCH DAWGS, AND YARD DAWGS

T he other day I saw something that bordered on the supernatural. There was a gigantic, matty-haired, black poodle riding in the back of a Silverado pickup truck. He was hanging his head around the side of the cab, his tongue and ears flapping in the wind. What bizarre things environment can do. Here's this normally aristocratic dog, whose breed is considered by most to be inherently arrogant, seemingly convinced he's a coonhound. I had a nearly uncontrollable urge to follow him home to see what sort of atmosphere could bring about this "I'm-jest-a-truck-ridin'-dawg" behavior in a poodle.

There are a great number of "truck-ridin' dawgs," such as coonhounds and retrievers. For that matter, pretty much any and all hunting dogs fall into that category. It's sort of an accepted fact that most "yard dawgs" are also "truck-ridin' dawgs," as are "porch dawgs." But poodles? I don't think so. That would be like taking a silky terrier hunting. I really have trouble conjuring up an unlaughable image of my cousin Andy hunting with the aid of a teacup poodle or a Shih Tzu. Nope. Andy's got "Buck" and "Hoss" (the chocolate labs), and "Elvis" (the singing coonhound). They are all true "huntin' dawgs"; and, as such, have earned the right to the rear of Andy's truck.

His daddy, my Uncle Henry, doesn't hunt anymore since he fell out of the deer stand and broke his tailbone in eleven places; so now his huntin' dawgs are just yard dawgs and porch dawgs. For those of you from north of the Mason-Dixon Line, please be advised that there is a *huge* difference between porch dawgs and yard dawgs. Clarence, the coonhound, is a "porch dawg," and understandably proud of that status. He and his sister Clarice are permanent residents of Uncle Henry's front porch. These elitists don't allow those "low-rent" yard dawgs ("Fescue" or "Prissy," the labs) anywhere near that front porch.

We still, at every family reunion, talk about the first time Aunt Pearl, Uncle Henry's wife, brought home "Pedro," the Chihuahua. He was a gift from one of Aunt Pearl's friends in her Women's Missionary Union group at Blackwater Baptist Church. Well, she brought that little, shivering speck of a dog home one night after a W.M.U. meeting, and put him in Uncle Henry's lap while he was

sleeping in his recliner. Uncle Henry didn't budge, so the wee
Pedro finally mustered up enough courage to slink up on Uncle
Henry's big, old belly and barrel chest, and lick him right smack
on his wide-open, snoring mouth. Uncle Henry opened his eyes in
sheer horror, screamed (in the highest of soprano-esque pitches)
"RAT!" as he sent that poor, pitiful, little dog flying across the
room. Thank heaven Aunt Pearl was able to catch him. (She
played shortstop for the Women's Baseball League during World
War II.)

Well, that little "Mexican rat-dawg" (as Uncle Henry called
him) became a serious bone of contention in their household.
Aunt Pearl was bound and determined that she was going to keep
her precious Pedro. Uncle Henry was just as determined that he
was not going to be humiliated in front of all his buddies at the
American Legion for having a "lap dawg" in his house. Well, the
problem was reconciled, much to Uncle Henry's further
mortification, a few months later when Prissy gave birth to a litter
of "lab-huahuas," not surprisingly among the ugliest dogs ever
born — they all got their Momma's big head and their Daddy's
miniature body (as puppies, this uneven weight distribution caused
them to topple over head-first a *whole* lot). Uncle Henry
threatened to kill Pedro *and* Prissy; and Aunt Pearl threatened to
never cook again if Uncle Henry made orphans of her "grand-
dawgs."

Ten years, 20 *coon*-huahuas and 46 *lab*-huahuas later, Pedro
pretty much rules the roost. He wields a tremendous amount of
power over all his considerably larger "women" (much more than
Uncle Henry does over Aunt Pearl). He also rides on a custom-
built platform Uncle Henry created for him in the back of his
pickup truck — wearing the black leather Harley-Davidson jacket
and spiked collar Uncle Henry bought him (just in case any of the
"boys" from the Legion see him). Yes, indeed, Pedro Cheeseman
has become the new standard-bearer for all non-hunting canines
who aspire to be "truck-ridin' dawgs" — both *very macho* pounds
of him.

WHAT THIS COUNTRY REALLY NEEDS
IS A SOUTHERN SOAP OPERA

T here are so many things about soap operas that drive me absolutely crazy. This being the case, you might ask, as my husband has on numerous occasions, "Well, why don't you just stop watching the stupid stuff?" It's because I am a bona fide, certifiable addict. That's why.

There really should be a twelve-step program: "Hi. My name is Rebel, and I'm a soapaholic."

I've learned that the soap gene is hereditary. My maternal grandmother passed it on to my mother, who passed it on to me. I have managed to shelter my teenaged daughters from the racier stuff, particularly the s-e-x! My gosh! I get more than a little uncomfortable watching these soap opera love scenes. You can see more skin in soaps nowadays than you can in a family-sized bag of pork rinds.

And the story lines are completely absurd. How many more times are we going to have to be subjected to that overused, brainless "*Who* am I? *Where* am I? *What* am I?" amnesiac plot? And, of course, these soap opera amnesiacs never seem to "come to" in an emergency facility. Forget that. It always has to be some slum alley in the midst of 500 junkies (and it helps, of course, if the amnesiac is wearing a full-length mink coat, a three-strand choker of cultured pearls, and a 12-carat diamond ring). Or, in an "inspired" twist on the old amnesia scenario, she will be mugged and robbed in an airport in Morocco, and nursed back to health and memory by a handsome, exotic, bachelor prince who adores her and wants to marry her and share his princedom with her (but this story line is effective only if the amnesiac is young and beautiful; if she'd been old and/or ugly, she'd still be at the airport — with a shaved head, and playing a tambourine). On yet another soap, the amnesiac (a wild and lusty woman before the memory fog overcame her) was found living among the Amish. ("Oh, my goodness! It seems I've completely forgotten how to shop, apply makeup, and mix a very dry martini. Oh, well. Besides, I find that I now much prefer a stinky, old, sway-backed horse and wooden buggy to a Mercedes.")

Soap opera writers, give us a break. No more amnesia, please. And no more of the equally tiresome, "I have absolutely no idea who the father of my baby is, but I've got it narrowed down to the

Yankees, the Red Sox, and the Lakers." These weak plots seem to always lead (in *real* life, what would be about 20 years, but in *soap* life, only two or three years) to what would be near incest, as the "baby" finds out the man she is about to marry is really her father and/or brother.

And another thing -- why are at least 90% of the characters on soaps so well off financially? They are, among other things, doctors, lawyers, psychiatrists, models, fashion designers, business tycoons, fashion photographers, heiresses, and best-selling authors. Maybe it's just the soaps *I* watch, but I can't recall ever seeing a mobile home on any of them, or anyone clipping coupons, or turning the lights off when they leave the room, or griping about the water bill, or ordering pizza, or sneaking their kids into drive-in movies in the trunk of their car, or putting leftovers in butter tubs, or going to Wal-Mart for the kids' back-to-school clothes. Or am I just mistaken? I don't think so. What I *am* seeing is maids, housekeepers, house "boys," and nannies whose employers don't ever "take a lick at a snake" (my Uncle Delroy's term for "work"). The folks in these soap opera houses don't cook, clean, pour their own coffee, or section their own grapefruit; and I guarantee you there's not a one of them who knows how to change a roll of toilet paper, let alone get a grass stain out of a soccer uniform, or dog wee-wee out of carpeting. But, then, I guess that's why those of us who can — and *do* — do all these things watch soaps in the first place — to escape, to fantasize, to envy, because, speaking for myself, what's on those soap operas resembles my life in no way at all. Nor do I even know anyone who lives like that. Then again, aren't they all set in either the north or in California? Well, *no wonder!*

What America really needs right now is a good, ol' Southern soap opera — and I'm not talking about "Dallas," either. Oil-rich jillionaires who move their whole families in with their mommas and daddies aren't exactly the norm down here. Instead of the Ewings and the Forresters, why not have a soap revolving around the poor but proud Butts family, the newest residents of the Elvis Presley Memorial Trailer Park in Nashville — the alcoholic father, Lonely; his long-suffering wife, Wavey; and their (yep, they're *really* his) kids, the 19-year-old technical school dropout, Jay-Del (short for James Delbert); the 18-year-old, "aspirin'-to-be-a-country-singin'-star," Shanda Rae; and the 13-year-old, "ballet-takin'" embarrassment to his daddy, but Wavey's "precious baby boy," Wiley. (His momma's working nights at the Pancake Parlor to pay for Wiley's ballet lessons, because his daddy wouldn't pay for them even if he could, which he can't, because he can't hold down a job ever since he knocked his eyes all wawnxy-jawed when he got "throwed" from the mechanical bull at the Cow Patty Bar ten years ago.) The other guys at the V.F.W. give Lonely the dickens about Wiley; but they believe Lonely when he tells them the boy's momma made him that way while Lonely was out in the Gulf working on those oil rigs for so long at a time. When he was working at the Alabama State Docks, he was home all the time, so "you don't see Jay-Del all pointy-toed in no lavender tights!" And Lonely said he's sure Shanda Rae isn't having any problems with her "sex-shul leanin's," either, because she wears her 18-pound, bleached-blonde hair just like her idol, Dolly Parton, and her jeans and shirts all fit skin-tight. According to Lonely, she "ain't nothin' but one-hunnert percent gal who shore ain't looking for nothin' but a *real* man, like Billy Ray Cyrus."

All the Buttses have moved to Nashville so that Shanda Rae can pursue her dream, and (according to Lonely and Wavey) buy them a "great, big, ol' ranch like Tanya Tucker's." Shanda Rae's their only hope, since Lonely (says he) can't work, Jay-Del won't work, and all of Wavey's tips go toward Wiley's ballet lessons and leotards.

And has anyone besides me ever noticed that there is never anyone watching television on "daytime dramas?" Talk about *unrealistic*. Are the writers trying to tell their soap's fans that the characters in the soap opera are too intelligent and/or refined to watch TV — unlike their fans, the "boobs" who obviously have no lives; and, consequently, nothing better to do than watch television? Maybe the writers of these soaps are the same ones who wouldn't let the Beav and the other '50s sitcom kids watch television.

Lonely and Wavey watch TV from the time they wake up 'til the time they fall asleep. Of course, Lonely hasn't mowed around the trailer in almost a year, and Wavey ran out of clean dishes a couple of months ago ("Well, wudjew thank paper plates was made for, anyhow?" she asks defensively); but, by golly, they both know how to change a roll of toilet paper all by themselves.

So you soap producers had better watch out, or you'll find "The Young and the Restless" has been replaced by the much more realistic "The Young and the *Wrestlers*." Or "Beverly *Hillbillies* 90210."

It could happen.

AINCHEW GONNA TAKE YOUR
CACKALATER TO HOLLOWLULU?

As much as I hate to admit it, there are some — well, okay — *lots* of Southerners who have a bit — okay — a *lot* of trouble with the King's English (or anyone else's, for that matter). For instance, there are those little-known (north of the Mason-Dixon Line) words "torge," "chard," and "chet."

"Torge," in a sense, means "in the direction of" — as in "Wylene, all slinky-like, moved torge DeWayne."

Then there's "chard," which has absolutely nothing to do with burning, but can refer to either a unit of measurement or to somewhere outside one's house, e.g., "Billy can't come in right now; he's rakin' the frun chard" (front yard). Or "I ain't believin' this! Alabama fumbled the dang ball on Auburn's ay-chard (eight-yard) line!"

And "chure," "chew," and "chet" are also very popular words down here. They're generally used with a lead-in word, such as "nah" or "ain," as in:

Daddy: "Son, ainchure momma got back from the K-Mart?"
Son: "Nawsir; nahchet."

AND

Momma: "Bubber, ainchew finished with your homework?"
Bubber: "Nawm. I ainchet."

A whole lot of folks down here speak "jew-ish" — not *yidd*-ish, *jew*-ish — even if they're Baptist, Methodist, Catholic, or have no religion at all. I think most Southerners speak jew-ish without even realizing it. For instance, there's "Win-jew," as in "Win-jew git back?" And then there's "How-jew," as in "How-jew do that?" There's "Wud-jew," as in "Now, wud-jew have to go and do that for?" But my personal favorite is "Why-jew," as in "Why-jew drank 'at lice Bud-wazzer ("Why did you drink that last Budweiser?")?"

In probably every other region of the United States, the word "kindly" means "having or showing kindness," but we Southerners know it also means "sort of," e.g., "Aint Texie's feelin' kindly poorly," or "It's been kindly a long time since we seen her," or "The hurricane kindly fizzled out."

In New York City, you're likely to freeze your hiney off if you go outside in 10° weather "buck-naked." In Ozark, Alabama, the same thing would happen at 30°, except you'd be "butt nekkid."

I have to admit, I have never understood the term "buck naked." I looked up the word "buck" (I already know what "naked" means) in my dictionary and found it defined (in part) as "The male of certain animals . . . . 2. A dandy, fop. 3. A young man . . . ." Well, I don't know of any male animals that don't run around naked pretty much all the time; but, then again, so do female animals. Consequently, that part of the definition doesn't help me understand the term "buck naked" any better than I did before.

The second part of the definition of "buck" describes it (or him) as "a dandy; (or a) fop." Now, when I hear or see the words "dandy" and/or "fop," the first two guys (and I use the term loosely) who come to mind are Boy George and The Artist Formerly Known as Prince (or, at our house, "The Little Purple One"), and I don't want to even *think* about either of them naked!

So that leaves the third definition, "A young man." Well, can a young man possibly be any nakeder (more naked?) than, say, an old man — or a young woman, or, for that matter, an old woman? I don't think so.

"Butt nekkid," on the other hand, needs no clarification.

That just goes to show, once again, that we Southerners might not always say it *right*, but we sure do quite often have a knack for saying it *better*.

Granted, there are some words with which Southerners don't do quite as well. For example, "Hawaii" comes out of my Aunt Claudelle's mouth, "How-ah-ya." Its capital, of course, is "Hollow-lulu." And my Uncle Colvin never goes to the Sack and Save without his "cackalater." After cooking all week long, Aunt Claudelle says Uncle Alvis is going to have to make do with "leffovers" on "Sairdy" (the day before Sunday).

I'll never forget the looks on the faces of Walt and Louise Giordano, the New Yorker parents of our neighbors, when we all went to the Interstate Fair in Pensacola several years ago. Their facial expressions were a mixture of fear, revulsion, and total bewilderment as they looked at a young man standing on a platform on the midway. He had what many Southerners refer to as "summer teeth" — you know, "some're here, some're there." (That happens a lot with the incest-inclined.) He was covered with snake and iguana tattoos. In his hands was a huge, yellow snake, which he held aloft as he yelled at passersby, "Cum an' gitcher pitcher took wif a ree-yull lav snike!" (Translation: "Come and get your picture taken with a real, live snake!") For whatever reason, we all passed on that golden opportunity.

One of the things that bothers many of us Southerners most when we see a Southerner portrayed on screen by, say, a Northerner — or even a Californian, isn't what's usually a dreadful "overdrawl"; it's when the pseudo-Southerner, whether male or female, walks up to one person, i.e., a person with no other persons around, and says, "How are *y'all*?" "Y'all" is a contraction (or, as Aunt Claudelle says, "contraption") for "you all," meaning two or more. It can be used to refer to people, horses, lovebugs, mosquitoes — anything, for that matter, that comes in two or more; but never, never, never *one*! That would be like having "a grit" for breakfast. It simply cannot be done that way.

And if you want to include an entire group in your "y'all," then you'd go to the superplural "all y'all," as in "We want all y'all to come on down here for Christmas."

I've been teased unmercifully for years by my non-Southern college classmates, co-workers and friends for saying "fixin' to," e.g., "I'm fixin' to go to the mall" or "It's fixin' to rain." It's never "fix*ing* to"; it's always "fix*in'* to." I've chosen to teach myself to say "pro-*gram*" instead of "pro-*grum*" and even "*wo*-mun" instead of "*waw*-mun," but "fixin' to" ain't fixin' to leave my vocabulary, thank you very much.

Besides, should I be intimidated by anyone who swims in the "Golf" of Mexico, drinks "melk," and eats "PEE-can PRAY-leens in their puh-JAM-uhs?" I don't think so.

```
┌─────────────────────────────────────────────────────┐
│                                                       │
│   HOLIDAYS:  BRIBERY, GRINCHES,                       │
│   AND A THERMOS OF GRITS                              │
│                                                       │
└─────────────────────────────────────────────────────┘
```

I HEREBY RESOLVE
TO MAKE NO RESOLUTIONS

H ere it is — another brand-new year! The slate is wiped
clean! It's time for fresh starts and new beginnings! Today
is the first day of the rest of our lives! Yeah, well, so is tomorrow.
Call me cynical; call me pessimistic; call me apathetic. Call me to
tell me you'll clean for me, do my laundry, and cook all my
family's meals for the next twelve months. All I know is that, for
the first time in as long as I can remember, I absolutely refuse to
make any New Year's Resolutions. I'm hopeless.

Hello. My name is Rebel, and I'm an unresolutable.

It's not that I haven't tried. Last year, for the eleventh year
running, I resolved to lose weight, exercise, start cooking more
(okay, start cooking *period*), improve my memory, be more
patient, stop procrastinating, keep up with my mountains of
laundry, improve my memory, stop wasting money, stop watching
so much television, and improve my memory. I was so filled with
hope. *This* time, I was really going to make it all happen. It didn't
matter that all the resolutions I had made in the prior years had
fallen through by January 3rd; *this* year was going to be different.
Well, it was different, all right. I gained weight faster. I joined a
gym, but couldn't find any exercise clothes that I would actually
leave the house in. I did actually start cooking more often, but quit
at my family's request. I put off stopping the procrastination until
I couldn't remember that I had wanted to stop in the first place. I
got totally fed up — real fast — with trying to be patient. I got so
tired of washing the same clothes over and over that I just went out
and bought a bunch of new ones (thereby terminating the "wasting
money" resolution, as well). And I bought a big-screen TV; so
now I'm not only watching *more* TV, I'm watching it *bigger*.

I guess I've just come to the point in my life where I've
accepted myself for what I am — a middle-aged woman with a big
rear end who's allergic to sweat. And I've reconciled myself to the
fact that Scarlett O'Hara is to blame for my procrastination

problem — she and that "I'll-think-about-that-tomorrow" obsession. As for the laundry, well, what in the world good does it do to wash, dry, fold, hang, and put away all those clothes? Somebody just turns right around and wears them again. As my Mamaw used to say, "With all this laundry, we're either the dirtiest folks in town, or the cleanest."

I guess I procrastinate about the laundry more than anything else.

"I just wore my last pair of clean socks today," my husband announced over his sardine-and-pineapple-cream-cheese sandwich (I've sort of procrastinated about going to the grocery store, too.).

"Wal-Mart's open," I replied, just like I always do.

"Mom, I think my paper cut's getting infected," announced Chelsea. "Do we have any antibiotic?"

"It's in the breadbox," I replied.

"I'm really afraid to ask, but why is it in the *breadbox*?" she asked.

"Because we're out of room in the medicine cabinet," I answered.

"But why the breadbox?"

"So that I could remember where it was," I responded.

"That doesn't make a whole lot of sense, Mom," she informed me.

"Of course, it does. The bread is moldy; therefore, it's covered with penicillin. Penicillin is an antibiotic; ergo, the antibiotics are together," I reasoned.

"Great. So I'm eating a penicillin-sardine-and-pineapple-cream-cheese sandwich," Les unhappily determined.

"*Ewwwww! Gross!*" the girls shrieked.

This is the thanks I get for trying to keep my family healthy and save money on prescription drugs at the same time. Living with a bunch of ingrates like this, it's no wonder I can't keep any resolutions!

NATIONAL AMNESTY DAY FOR HUSBANDS (A/K/A VALENTINE'S DAY)

V alentine's Day should be seen as a day of redemption for many husbands. After having given their wives Christmas gifts chosen from the pathetic dregs remaining in department/discount/grocery stores at 5:30 P.M. on Christmas Eve, they have (only six weeks later) an undeserved opportunity to restore their good standing with their spouses.

Stores, their stocks replenished after Christmas, abound with jewelry, cashmere sweaters, perfumes — truly convincing ways for husbands to say, "Please forgive me for giving you those nose-hair clippers for Christmas. There was nothing else left in the store — *really*."

Granted, some husbands give their wives special gifts for Christmas, Valentine's Day, anniversaries, and at any and all times, special occasion or not — but not my neighbor's husband, Matt.

Over the years, Matt has bestowed upon his wife Ellen such "romantic" gifts as a weedeater, a Buttmaster® (totally *un*requested and *un*appreciated), a socket set, and (my personal favorite) a musical camouflage toilet seat (because you never know *when* deer will come into the bathroom). That's why I was so completely surprised to receive a frantic call from Matt the other day seeking my help with the selection of Ellen's Valentine's Day gift.

"You mean she's still upset about that lovely electric plunger-and-toilet-brush set you gave her for Christmas?" I asked. "How could she not appreciate that?"

My sarcasm was totally lost on this man.

"I know! I still can't believe it myself. But last week she finally started talking to me again, at least. I guess this time I just need to try to get her something, you know, *womanish*," he admitted, seeming to actually, at last, see the light. "Can you help me, . . . please?"

Matt picked me up on Saturday, the day before Valentine's Day, and we headed for the mall.

"Do you have anything special in mind?" I asked, obviously without thinking.

"How about socks?" he proposed enthusiastically.

"*Socks?*"

"Yeah. She wears socks — a lot."

"Well, why don't we try to find something a little more, uh . . . special. Like maybe earrings or perfume"

"She already has earrings. And I just got her that gallon bottle of Monkey Magnolia perfume at the drugstore a couple of years ago. Believe it or not, she still has almost the whole bottle left."

"Imagine that! Well, then this time, why don't we try to find something a little less . . . *exotic* than Monkey Magnolia?" I recommended as I led him to the perfume counter of one of the nicer department stores, and let him sniff the scents as the clerk sprayed them on the cards.

"How about this one?" I suggested. "It's lovely."

"Yeah. It's okay; but don't you have something a little more . . . *piney*? You know, like the little trees that hang from rearview mirrors?" he asked the clerk. "I really like those."

"We do not *do* 'piney', sir," she answered, looking at him in absolute disbelief.

"Gosh, I'm sorry," Matt said to me as I quickly dragged him away. "I guess I just don't know that much about perfume. And all those bottles are just so *little*. Can't we find her something *bigger*?"

"Matt, regardless of what you and most other men tend to think, bigger is not always better. How about if we look for something for her in a lingerie shop? Most women love dainty, feminine lingerie."

"*Lingerie*? You mean like *underwear*?" he screeched painfully. "You actually want *me* to go into one of those . . . those *bra* and *panty* stores! *No way*! The pictures of those models in there are almost . . . well, they're practically *pornographic*! And I've seen how they dress those mannequins! Well, heads or no heads, they're just wearing a little bit of elastic and lace! Ellen couldn't even get into those scraps of . . . stuff. She wears cotton drawers, and she's got real big . . . I mean, she's too . . . *chesty* for those . . . those little pieces of . . . . Nope! Just forget it! Besides, married men do *not* go into those places — especially with someone else's wife! I'm not going in there! She's *got* underwear! A man can't buy his wife . . . *underwear*, for cryin' out loud!"

The poor guy was shaking at about a 7.5 on the Richter Scale at that point. I knew I had to calm him down before he imploded.

"Well, then how about a nice sweater or a blouse?"

"Nah, she's already got a sweater and a blouse. I've got to get her something she doesn't already have."

Pulling up in front of my house after eight hours of shopping, and with absolutely nothing at all to show for it except aching feet, I grudgingly resigned myself to the fact that this man was completely hopeless.

"I'm really sorry I couldn't help you, Matt," I apologized.

"Hey, that's all right," he reassured me. "Shoot, I still have nearly a whole *hour* before the Hardware Supercenter closes."

The Hardware Supercenter. That great repository of "*womanish.*"

We in the neighborhood have yet to learn exactly what Matt gave Ellen for Valentine's Day this year. Whatever it is, she's obviously not very happy with it because Matt's been sleeping in their backyard every night — in thermal underwear with butt flap (Ellen's 1993 gift from Matt), camouflage hunting suit (1987), plaid flannel hunting cap with fleece flaps (circa 1990), warmed by a kerosene heater (Valentine's Day, 1990) — in the deer stand (Mother's Day, 1994). To insure that Matt doesn't come down until *she's* good and ready for him to, she's standing guard with her 40th birthday present from Matt — a romantic pellet gun.

Aim for that butt flap and *fire*, girlfriend!

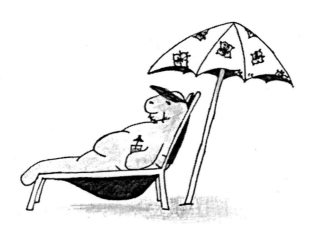

THE DAY THE RABBIT DIED

E aster just hasn't been the same around our house since the rabbit died — not the one at the obstetrician's office. I'm talking about the one who brought the Easter baskets for the kids. We killed the old fellow off when our first-born daughter turned ten. That's when I (at the behest of their daddy) took her to a nice restaurant for a "Mommy/Daughter Lunch," and not only cleared the air about Santa, the Tooth Fairy, and the Easter Bunny, but the "birds and the bees," as well. I didn't feel the need to go into great detail on the s-e-x thing; but I quickly learned that I would've been much better off elaborating about that particular issue. I was totally out of my element with the "bunny thing."

"So, you mean you and Daddy have been *fibbing* to us this *whole* time?" Carly asked in disbelief.

"Well, honey, we didn't exactly *fib*. We just . . . ."

"Let me get this straight," she broke in. "You're saying that there isn't now, nor has there *ever been*, an Easter Bunny. Right?"

"Well, yes. I guess that's what I'm saying . . . ," I stammered.

"So, for all these years, just whose lap was it that I've been sitting on at the mall?"

"Those were just people dressed up as the Easter Bunny, sweetheart."

"Total strangers, you mean. Does Chelsea know about any of this — Santa, the Tooth Fairy, the Rabbit?" she inquired about her younger sister.

"No, honey. She's still too young. We'll tell her when she's ten, like I'm doing with you now.

"Hmmmmm," she murmured, rubbing her chin, and with that mercenary look that always gives me the bejeebers creeping onto her normally angelic little face.

"Suppose . . . ," she continued, "just *suppose* somebody *accidentally* spilled the beans and told her the truth about all these guys."

"You *wouldn't!*" I exclaimed.

"Of course, I wouldn't . . . if the price is right," the little money-grubber replied.

"How much?" I mumbled, ashamed at having given in.

"How about three bucks, a chocolate shake, and a pinkie-promise that I won't have to wear that dumb hat and those goofy ruffled socks and patent leather shoes on Easter Sunday."

"How about three bucks, a chocolate shake, you wear the shoes and socks, and I'll give in on the hat," I countered.

"Poor little Chelsea. Imagine having all your childhood fantasies destroyed . . . in one fell swoop," she threatened, with the sweetest smile on her face and her eyelashes aflutter.

"*All right*! *All right*!" I relented. "I won't make you wear the socks, but you still have to wear the shoes."

"Oh, Mom. They're so *dorky*!"

"What's wrong with those shoes?"

"Well, for one thing, they *buckle*!"

"And your point *is*?" I asked.

"My point is that now that I know all about . . . . Well, *you* know . . . . Well, I just think I should be able to wear something *grownier*."

"*Grownier*? Like what?" I asked.

"Like . . . pantyhose and shoes with heels," she responded.

"Get *out*!" I nearly yelled. "You're just ten minutes into the Bursting of the Bunny Myth. You can't possibly expect to be able to wear *pantyhose* and shoes with *heels*!"

"Here comes Santa Claus! Here comes Santa Claus, right down Santa Claus Lane . . . ," she began singing.

"*All right*! *All right*! You can wear pantyhose," I gave in, more ashamed than ever. "But they've got to be thick — and *no* heels!"

She finished her chocolate shake and clutched her $3.00, smiling as we rode home in silence.

As I walked by her room, I heard the following conversation:

"So, how'd it go?" Chelsea asked.

"It went *great*!" Carly replied. "Here's your dollar."

"*Hey*! That three bucks was *my* idea!" Chelsea argued. "Where's my other 50 cents?"

Imagine their surprise when I opened the door and took back *my* $3.00. And they both looked *so* cute on Easter Sunday in their little outfits — complete with hats, dorky patent leather shoes, and goofy ruffled socks.

The Rabbit is *dead*! *Long live The Momma*!

THE GHOSTS
OF HALLOWEENS PAST

M aybe it was because we didn't have a whole lot of money when I was a little girl, or maybe it was just because back in the "olden days" (as my kids refer to my childhood/youth), one couldn't *easily* find ready-to-wear costumes for kids; but I can remember spending many Halloween nights trick-or-treating in a white sheet with eyeholes, fashioned expressly by my mother so that I could see where I was going. On those Halloweens when I wasn't a ghost, I was a gypsy, pirate, hobo, or angel (the most appropriate of all costumes, if I must say so myself — and I guess I must). These were all simple costumes —and really cheap, too.

My how things have changed. These days, kids have to be Mulan or Baby Spice; or they have to have an $80 latex mask of that terrifying, grotesque, skeletal slasher from the movie "Scream." All these are trendy, pricey, soon-to-be-discarded costumes that the kids wouldn't *dream* of being seen in next year. For whatever reason, they just aren't content being regular ghosts anymore. I thought that with the release of the movie "Casper, the Friendly Ghost," there might come a simultaneous return of that extinct Halloween symbol. No such luck. The kids who show up at my door on Halloween night are arrayed as everything from a dead football player (complete with a hatchet buried in his bloody helmet) to his girlfriend, the zombie cheerleader (bullet hole graphically displayed in her forehead), to Dolly Parton (complete with high-heeled "mules," big hair, and even bigger . . . , well, *you know*.)

I can assure you, from vast personal experience, that these costumes are definitely not white sheets with eyeholes. It's totally mind-boggling to think of the inordinate amount of money spent on some of these costumes — most of which are worn for about two hours on very dark Halloween nights — not to mention the time spent agonizing over "what to be" on that particular night.

Here's the scenario at our house on the eve of Halloween last year:

"Well, what are you two going to be for Halloween?" I asked my daughters, innocently enough.

"*BE*? What can we possibly *BE*? Everything good has already been taken," my first-born wailed.

"She's right, Mom. There's just nothing left *to* be anymore," agreed her sister.

"Well, of course there is, girls. I've got some great ideas! How about being pirates or hobos — or angels — or, *novel idea* — ghosts?" I suggested, brimming over with excitement, truly impressed with my boundless creativity, and, above all, hoping not to have to spend big bucks on costumes.

"Oh, Mom, *get real!*" Carly moaned. "Nobody wears those corny costumes anymore."

"Corny? *CORNY?* Since when is being a ghost for Halloween corny?" I asked, with my little feelings more than slightly hurt.

"Like *since you* were a little kid, Mom," responded Chelsea, my painfully truthful child.

"That's true, Mom. No offense, but those are just pretty retarded costumes for this day and age," Carly added.

"So, what you're saying is that back during the Civil War, when I was a child, it was okay to wear them; but in this, the day of the Jetsons, E.T., and Star Trek, it's just not even thinkable?"

"The Jetsons, E.T., and Star Trek? Mom, no self-respecting kid would ever wear those goofy, dated, old costumes. They've been out of style for, like, *years*," Carly informed me, rolling her eyes at her sister. This eye rolling is "teenage-ese" for "Our mother's a certifiable nerd, but just humor her. We'll be away at college soon."

"Well, then you two come up with something better," I sulked.

"That's just it, Mom. There *isn't* anything! Maybe you should just resign yourself to the fact that we're getting too old for costumes," Chelsea advised me.

I think I could actually *hear* my heart break when she said that.

When each of them turned ten, I had dutifully taken them out for a mother-daughter lunch at a really nice restaurant, where I set about excruciatingly 'fessing up to the truth about Santa, the Easter Bunny, the Tooth Fairy, and PeeWee Herman. We also had the obligatory and unbelievably uncomfortable (for me, anyway) "birds-and-bees" talk. (I learned a lot.)

I just wasn't ready to give up Halloween, too. This was the last bastion of their childhood. They play "Spin the Bottle" at parties, for crying out loud! Isn't there something I can hold on to? Some teeny, little fragment of their rapidly-departing childhood?

They had been Barbie, Jasmine, My Little Pony, Donald Duck, the Little "Mermworm," Freddy Krueger, and even Dead Jed Clampett. I wanted to do the sheet thing, DAGNABBIT! It is every mother's inherent right to do the sheet thing for Halloween! I had *never*, as a mommy, done the sheet thing.

I begged and pleaded. I even laid on the guilt — *thickly*.

"Just this one last time, dress up for Mommy! Be ghosts! PLEEEEASE!

"My shameless appeals were met with what I interpreted as less than enthusiasm.

Well, desperate times call for desperate measures.

"For $20 each?" I bribed.

"Make it *$50*, and you've got a deal," they harmonized.

"*Okay* — $50," I agreed hastily. I had no shame. I had no pride. Soon, I would have no money.

"Cool," they both agreed.

That was when I discovered how truly rare a commodity a white sheet is nowadays. My girls looked so cute, though. One plaid ghost and one floral ghost — with absolutely perfect eyeholes.

And no one else — anywhere in town — had costumes quite like theirs. And relatively cheap — only $100 cash and two ruined sets of Laura Ashley sheets.

But I WON!

I think.

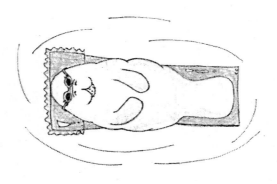

TURKEYS I HAVE KNOWN

T he word "turkey" just doesn't mean what it used to. For
instance, in 19_7_7, "turkey" conjured up pleasant thoughts of a
bountiful Thanksgiving dinner with the extended family. This
dinner generally consisted of the aforementioned turkey, along
with sweet potato casserole, sweet (not *English*) peas, cornbread
dressing (never, never, *never* "stuffing" — in the Deep South,
stuffing is what you're *doing* at the table, not what you're *eating*
there), cranberry sauce, broccoli casserole, cloverleaf dinner rolls,
sweet iced tea, and pecan (puh-*cahn'*, not *pee'*-can) pie.

In 19_8_7, the word "turkey" signified an "especially senseless"
person. When one heard the word "turkey," one didn't auto-
matically think of the colossal bird. One usually associated a
turkey with someone to whom one might say, "You *turkey*, you
can't milk that bull!" (*Not* a compliment.)

In l9_9_7, it's a totally 'nother thing. "Turkey" tends to bring to
mind dividing Thanksgiving Day between families, or eating in a
restaurant.

This year, we politely declined our neighbors' invitation to join
them for Thanksgiving dinner. He's from The Netherlands; she's
from London. They're serving filet mignon. Nice meal — on any
other occasion. Actually, I love filet mignon. I'm not a
vegetarian, nor do I ever aspire to be; but there's just something
almost sacrilegious about *not* having turkey for Thanksgiving. I
have an inexplicable foreboding that Miles Standish or one of the
other Pilgrims will come back from the dead, and put me on the
rack or something if I fail to eat turkey for Thanksgiving. It's like
not having black-eyed peas and hog jowls for New Year's Day —
bad luck will plague you for the entire year if you don't eat them.
(Actually, I substitute a nice pork tenderloin for the jowls. There's
just something about eating the flabby underjaws of a pig that I
find extremely repulsive — maybe it's just me.) But I really feel
that something terribly frightful will happen if I don't eat turkey
for Thanksgiving. Something like the Black Plague, . . . or orange
will become "the" color for spring, . . . or disco will become
popular again, or . . . Jerry Springer will be elected President of the
United States, or . . . . Well, that last one is definitely the worst-
case scenario I can come up with, anyway.

I'm not taking any chances. I'm eating turkey for Turkey Day.
And if my family's really lucky, my father-in-law will cook it. In
20 years of marriage, I've been called upon only once to cook

turkey and dressing. For one thing, no one bothered to tell me it takes *two months* for a 40-pound frozen turkey to thaw. For another, no one told me there's no residential oven on God's green earth that will even *cook* a 40-pound turkey. And, for another, no one informed me that cornbread dressing really shouldn't be the consistency of orange juice. Like I was *born* knowing these things. And *giblets* — well, I had absolutely no idea what the nasty little things even *were*, much less that they belonged in gravy. Nor did anyone even suggest to me that giblet gravy should be relatively smooth, except for the giblets.

Mine was the consistency of . . . well, do you remember Silly Putty®? My giblet gravy *couldn't* be poured, and it *wouldn't* be ladled. It *could* be sort of "pulled."

At least it didn't go to waste. After dinner, the kids pressed it onto the Sunday comics and made some really good copies. Then they had a "gravy pull," which, from what I understand, is pretty much the same as a *taffy* pull, except that people will actually *eat* taffy after it's been pulled.

When the kids couldn't even force feed my gravy to the dogs, they rolled it into a sphere and played a little softball with it. Well, it might not taste good, but man does that stuff get *airborne*!

I'm thinking: Giblet Flubber $$$$$$!!!!

GRINCHES IN TRAINING

My husband brought down the last of the 87 boxes of Christmas decorations from the attic. After that, he wasn't in a very good mood. For whatever reason, he doesn't share my enthusiasm for hauling out all the wreaths, garland, ornaments, bows, Santas, nativity scenes, and strings and strings of miniature lights. He is the original Christmas-stealing "Grinch." It's not that he doesn't enjoy the holiday and the festivities. It's just that he *abhors* putting up the decorations. That's second only to taking them down.

"I'm not doing *anything* this year except the outside lights," he announced.

"Fine," I agreed.

"Well, I'm *not*."

"I heard you, honey."

"You and the girls can do all that Martha Stewart stuff," he declared. "I'm not getting into any of that. I'm not going to do those frou-frou things in the house with all the ribbons and candles and glittery stuff and all."

"Okay."

"And the *tree*. I'll help you put up the tree and the lights on it — but just on the top part that you can't reach."

"That's nice, sweetie."

"And the *angel*. I'll put the angel on top. And whatever ornaments you all can't reach. I don't want you or the girls to fall," he stated.

"Thank you, love," I told him.

"Well, I guess I can hang the garland in the foyer. That's got to be done on the ladder, you know."

"Yes, I do know that, honey. Thank you."

"But I'm definitely *not* going to *decorate*, so don't expect me to do that," he emphasized as the girls and I continued to take everything out of the boxes.

"I don't, dear. I never expect that."

"Good. Because I'm not."

Two hours later, happy Christmas carols emanated from the stereo while the two younger Grinches-in-training bemoaned their slavery.

"Mom, we've got too much *stuff*," whined one.

"Christmas will be *over* before we get all this up," added her sister.

"Oh, girls, why can't you just get into the spirit of the season and enjoy decorating the house? Christmas is over before we even know it. Delight in it while you can," I implored them.

"I'd delight in it more if someone else did all this decorating," lamented Carly.

"Okay. That's fine. If you really feel that way, you two just go and do whatever you'd like. I'll do it all myself."

"No, we'll help," said Carly. "If we don't, you'll pout."

"Pout? *Pout*? *Me*? I do *not* pout," I advised her.

At this point, she and her sister both burst into laughter, as did their father from his non-decorating position on the living room sofa.

"Well, I *don't*," I whimpered.

"Okay, Mom. If you say so," said Chelsea, looking out the window. "Uh-oh, the Dixons are unloading their tree. Good grief, it's *huge*!"

"*Huge*?" I inquired, sprinting to the window. "*How* huge?"

"Looks to me like about a . . . a twelve-footer, Mom," she answered, with trepidation in her voice and fear in her eyes as she realized her mistake. "But I could be wrong. You know how I am with measurements. It really may just look that long because their car is so short. That's probably it! I'm sure . . . ."

"*Twelve feet*? It *can't* be twelve feet!" I exclaimed. "She told me they were going to use their eight-foot *artificial* tree! She can't *do* this to me! Oh, my *gosh*! Look at that thing! It's *at least* twelve feet tall! And by the time they get that tacky two-foot camel on the top of it, it'll make ours look like an *azalea bush*! Get up, honey! We've got to get to the tree lot!"

"What are you talking about? We're not getting another tree. You just bought this tree. This is the one you just *had* to have. It's eleven feet tall — and I'm not going anywhere," he asserted.

Silly boy.

"But it's *fake* and the Dixons' tree is *real*! And theirs is at least a foot taller than ours," I told him.

"Need I remind you that you said you didn't *want* a real tree? After vacuuming Christmas tree needles last year, you said you'd never have another real tree. Besides, this is a beautiful tree. And you've already decorated it," he reminded me.

"I don't care! I'll just *un*decorate it. She did this *intentionally*! She just waited until I got mine up, and then turned around and went out and got a bigger one! That shrew! She's *so* competitive! What's her problem?"

Les, Carly and Chelsea looked at each other and rolled their eyes.

"We'll be waiting in the van, Daddy," Carly said.

"I'll get the keys," he relented.

We returned from the Christmas tree lot seven hours later with our new tree. I'm not sure how we even got it home. We just laid it lengthwise on the roof of the car, and tied the top of it somewhere under the front axle. Les hung out the driver's side window in an attempt to see where he was heading, while Chelsea stuck her head out the passenger's side, directing him as best she could. I sat in the trunk of our car, holding onto the trunk of my precious tree, while waving curious and furious drivers around our creeping vehicle.

Carly, all the while, was slumped down on the back floorboard, murmuring something about moving to Japan to live with her Auntie Dee.

Teenagers.

We finally got the replacement tree home, and called on several neighbors (except for the *Dixons*, of course) to help us unload it and get it into the house.

"Is this thing going to even *fit* in your living room?" asked Doubting Tom, from down the street.

"Of course, it will," I responded.

"Nope," said my husband, ever the pessimist.

"Nope," said Chelsea, the pessimist's younger child.

"Nope," said Carly, the deserter. "Mom, can I stay at Nicole's 'til Christmas?"

"Nope," I informed her. "This tree is going to be the most beautiful one we've ever had!"

"She says that every year, doesn't she?" asked Bob, the Neighbor Who Knows Too Much and Remembers All of It.

"Yep," answered Les.

I glared at them. They shut up.

"So, do any of you guys want to stay and help us set 'er up?" I inquired.

"Gotta mow the lawn," said Todd.

"It's *December*, Todd. The grass is dead," I reminded him.

"I meant . . . chop some firewood," he said. "*Yeah*, that's it. I've gotta chop some firewood."

"I've got to watch the kids," stated Dave.

"You don't *have* any kids," I notified him.

"You can watch *my* kids, Dave," Todd volunteered.

"Thanks, man," Dave said. "I've got to watch Todd's kids, Rebel. Otherwise, I'd be glad to do it. Really."

"Sure, Dave," I responded.

They disappeared like I had asked them to make a run to the store for feminine products.

So, we, the nuclear family, were left on our own to undecorate the fake tree, and start decorating the "real" tree.

"We're going to need more decorations. We're a foot short," I moaned at 3:00 the following morning.

"No! No more decorations! Just . . . *stretch* those," suggested my husband.

"What do you mean 'stretch' these?"

"I mean, just put more space between the decorations."

"You mean just leave huge, gaping *holes* between them! I can't do that," I informed him. "Come on, we've got to buy more decorations!"

"*No!* I'm not going anywhere," he declared. "There are plenty of decorations on that tree. Just move them around some. Or, better yet, get the girls to make some of those paper chains and snowflakes."

"Forget it, Dad. We've made our share of paper chains and snowflakes — no more!" Carly informed him.

"Besides, those all go on the 'children's tree,'" said Chelsea. "This one is Mom's 'designer' tree. This is her 'just-you-try-to-make-yours-look-better-than-*this*-Donna-Dixon' tree. You'd better just go with us to get more decorations, Dad."

"It's *three* in the morning, for Pete's sake. There's nothing even open now," he protested.

"Oh, yes, there is," I advised him. "Holiday-O-Rama is open *24/7!* Put on your jackets and gloves, everybody! We're *off!*"

That's when I'm sure I heard him say, "But none of us more so than you, honey."

I MISS TOYS "R" US®

M *om! Where's my Christmas list?* yelled my older daughter.
"Why?" I asked, hope filling my voice. "Are you crossing something off?"

"No, *silly*. I've just typed up an addendum for it."

"Great. We don't really have to eat for the rest of the month," I sighed.

"Oh, Mom. You have such a flair for the dramatic. Besides, it's only a few things. Well, actually, it's probably more like *several* things. You see, the ones with four stars by them are the ones I really, really just absolutely *have* to have. Three stars indicate the ones I could live without, but it would be pretty difficult. Two stars are the ones that would make me very happy; and the ones with just one star would show me just how much you love me, since they're the ones I want the least — but still would be more complete having," she informed me as she handed me the three typed, single-spaced pages to add to the nine she had already given me. With just one quick glance, I realized there are fewer stars in the Milky Way than there were on those sheets of paper.

"Mom," said her younger sister as she entered the room, "you can just tear up the old list I gave you."

"The 'old' list?" I asked.

"Yes, ma'am. That was the one I made before I turned 13. There were some pretty childish things on there. I don't even want them anymore. I really do need more mature things now."

"Chelsea, honey, you just turned 13 yesterday. Do 24 hours really make that much difference?" I asked.

"Oh, *no!*" she shrieked. "That means you've already bought me all the goofy stuff on that other list, doesn't it?"

"Sweetie, that list was seven pages long, and I just got it from you last week," I assured her. "So, no, I haven't even *begun* shopping from it."

"Thank goodness. That scared me *so* bad! I could just see me going back to school the week after Christmas with stuff for a *12-year-old*," her newfound maturity evident in her voice. "Anyway, you'll be glad to know that this list is only six pages long."

"Yep," I responded. "That's going to make my life a whole lot simpler. Thank you."

"You're welcome," she replied, handing me her six-page, single-spaced catalog. "Oh, by the way, I thought that star system might be a little too confusing for you, so my list is just in order from number 1 to number 264 — with number one being the thing I most can't do without. But, of course, that doesn't mean that I wouldn't be just as happy with number 264 as I would with, say, 30 or even 55. So, just remember that I'm not expecting every, single thing on my list. Gosh, I'm not even expecting *half* those things. Wouldn't that make me a greedy little toot? Besides, I'm 13 now. It would be terribly *childish* of me to expect *everything*. So, just remember, precious, wonderful, beautiful, best-momma-in-the-world, when you take that list with you when you go shopping, just remember which of your two daughters loves you more. That would be me, the *un*greedy one."

"Oh, *please*!" groaned her 14-and-a-half-year-old sister. "That child has absolutely no shame. She is *so* obvious! And how about that crack about my star system confusing you. If that isn't a slap in the face, I don't know what is. Just because you're turning 50 in a month, she thinks you can't fathom a system of stars. That is *so* unbelievably insulting and *ageist*, Mother. Besides, I listed the 'key' to my system at the bottom of each sheet, with asterisks to help you in case you forget. You know, four stars equal 'gotta have,' three stars equal . . . ."

"I've got it, dear. I think my poor, pickled, old momma-brain can comprehend both of your 'systems.' Now, please just let me have some time alone with these reams of paper you two have given me. That way I can choose between electricity and groceries for the month of January."

Gosh. This sure was easier when they were little. Barbie®, My Little Pony®, Cabbage Patch Dolls®; teddy bears, and trikes and bikes have been replaced by cashmere sweaters; $100 sunglasses; CDs by groups with names like Dr. Mr. Gangsta, Sir Rapalot, and Snoopy's Dog's Dog; $80/ounce perfume; $200 tennis shoes; aromatherapy candles guaranteed to expunge the stress experienced by 13-year-olds; and CD players so big they require a room of their own.

And, as sick as this may sound to those of you with small children, I really do miss Toys "R" Us. I never thought I'd say that, but it's true.

As ashamed as I am to admit it, last week at the mall I even tried to coerce Chelsea into sitting on Santa's lap — *one more time*. It's just that I saw all the other moms in line waiting for their kids to have their pictures made with Santa, and I felt left out. I begged and pleaded — to no avail. She did tell me, though, that if I could find Brad Pitt dressed in a Santa suit, she'd do it.

Shoot, if I could find Brad Pitt in a Santa suit at the mall, there'd be a 48" by 72" color photo on our mantle of *me* sitting on Santa Brad's lap, *grinnin' like a mule eatin' briars.*

IN PURSUIT OF BARBIE®

M y heart bled a couple of years ago as I read about and saw on the national news all the poor mommies who had to go in search of the "dreaded, elusive Tickle-Me-Elmo®." I was amazed at how quickly my friends with young children turned on that once beloved and most adored of all the Sesame Street™ characters.

"I'd like to be left alone in a room with that little red fuzzwad for just *ten minutes*," seethed Melanie, mother of four-year-old twins.

"I wouldn't even need *that* long," countered Kathy, mother of Stephanie, an only child who doesn't even begin to comprehend the concept of "You can't have that."

"I know. I *hate* the little *creep*," said Judi, mother of four kids under seven years of age. "He's even made me hate the color red."

"Is it really that bad, guys?" I asked, pretending I had no idea what they were going through, but thinking, "Oh, if they only knew . . . ."

But none of them even had daughters during *"The Horrible Holiday Barbie® Shortage"* of 1990. Even the challenge of securing that little red demon doll Elmo pales in comparison with it.

I know it seems hard to believe, but I'm absolutely certain that every single momma at that particular Toys "R" Us® in Atlanta on that freezing November morning was pre-menstrual. Forget sisterhood. Forget world peace. Forget manners and civility. We were "women with a mission." And that mission was to get that stupid doll or die trying — or, for that matter — *kill* trying.

I was there when "THE" truck arrived at *4:30* that momentous morning. For waking at 2:45 A.M., I thought I should be nominated for saint(e)hood (*Mother* Rebel has a nice ring to it). However, that image of the saintly me faded as soon as I pulled into the parking lot at 4:00 A.M., and saw the 2,735 mommas who were already there.

"What a *horrible, selfish* mother I am," I thought as I sat there immobilized by guilt. "These women evidently camped out (the tents kind of tipped me off)."

The guilt of a mother overshadows all other guilt.

But that's an 18-wheeler. Surely, *surely*, it can easily hold at least 10,000 Barbies!

I felt confident. So I sat there on my blanket, sipping from my thermos of hot grits (it was really early when I tried to make coffee, and the grits and coffee canisters were side by side), reading my book by headlight, and shivering in the 22° blackness while the driver *ever so slowly* backed the trailer up to the loading dock.

The tension was so thick you could cut it with a knife as we sat there growling at each other like jealous Chihuahuas. We had no fear. We had no shame. We had no feelings in our extremities. We were . . . *IN PURSUIT OF BARBIE!*

Well, at 6:00 A.M., the doors to the store finally opened. What a terrifying sight we were. It was just like the crazy stampeding wildebeest scene from "The Lion King." It was all arms and legs and teeth, and pushing and shoving and maiming — and that was before we even got to the door.

Being near the back of the herd, I followed the screams to the doll aisle — it was even more frightful than I'd feared. Those women were *possessed*. They were loading themselves down with boxed Barbies, although the poor, little teenaged assistant manager was shrieking, "Ladies, *please*! There's a two-Barbie limit for each customer! Ladies! *Ladies!*"

"Oh, go tell your momma she needs you, you little wienie!" shouted one particularly rude and nasty crazy woman.

Within five minutes, there was not a Holiday Barbie left on the shelves. But *I* got *mine*. I have absolutely no idea how I did it, though. Everything was a blur. I think I've just managed to block it from my mind somehow. That happens a lot with trauma, from what I understand.

Unfortunately, the older and slower (and saner) moms didn't make it in time. Some were crying; others were cussing. Yet none of the hoarders even offered to share with them. And the assistant manager was too frightened to make a second attempt to enforce the limit. But I knew *my* little Barbie-loving daughter wouldn't be disappointed. And that made what I had gone through to get Barbie all worthwhile — the black eye, the frostbite, even the loose teeth.

Yes, it was all worth it. It was worth it, that is, until the morning after Christmas when I found Barbie on the front porch — *naked*, covered with frost, and sporting a huge bald spot.

Don't feel bad, Barbie. I know just how you feel. But it *could* be worse — at least *you've* got a waistline.

WHO SAYS CHRISTMAS IS THE MOST EXPEN$IVE HOLIDAY?.

L ast year at this time, I shamelessly bribed my teenaged daughters to wear ghost costumes for Halloween. They've just informed me, however, that there's not enough money in the paltry Covan "treasury" to persuade them to even *go* trick-or-treating, much less wear costumes.

"Mom, get real! I'm 15 years old and 5'4". Who's gonna even give *me* candy? I'll be laughed out of the neighborhood," Carly attempted to reason with me.

"She's right, Mom. You've just got to face it. We've *grown up*," my "baby," 13-year-old Chelsea, agreed.

"I told you girls not to ever use *those words* in this house," I scolded, looking up at both of them. "Besides, I can cover your faces, and no one will ever even know it's you."

"Not until they see you holding our hands and leading our way with a *flashlight* in your mouth," moaned Chelsea.

"I'll wear a mask, too!" I promised.

"It'll never work, Mom. The minute you take your flashlight out and open your mouth, everyone will know it's Psycho Mom and her Teenaged Toddlers," Carly countered.

"Mom, you've really got to let it go. We don't *want* to go trick-or-treating! We're too old and too big for Santa's knee. We know the truth about the Easter Bunny and the Tooth Fairy. You've just *got* to accept the fact that we're not little kids anymore."

I looked at Chelsea as she announced her Declaration of Adolescence, and could still see her at two years old, with her thumb in her mouth, grinning up at me around it. And as I looked at the too-mature Carly, I could see only a six-year-old with a blonde ponytail on the side of her head, dragging around the ever-present, bedraggled *Barbie-du-jour*, and wearing her adored New Kids On The Block T-shirt that dragged the ground.

"Well, then, what am *I* supposed to do for Halloween?" I asked with undisguised disappointment.

"You can just stay at home and give out candy, like the *normal* adult population," Carly suggested.

"Thrillsville," I pouted.

"Oh, come on, Mom. It'll be *fun*," urged Chelsea. "You'll have a great time just giving candy to all the cute little kids."

"No, I *won't*."

"You *will*. I *promise*," Carly attempted to assure me.

"I *won't*. I'll just want to be . . . *out there*."

"Well, Mom, we're really, really sorry to dash your hopes, but we're *not* going trick-or-treating," Carly informed me.

"*Fine*," I replied. "I'll just rent a couple of the neighborhood kids."

"Now, that's a *great* idea!" encouraged Chelsea.

"It was a *bluff*! Aw, come on, girls. Just one more time — for Mommy," I implored. "I'll make it worth your while."

They looked at each other, greed quickly winning out over embarrassment and humiliation.

"How much?" Carly, the mercenary one, asked.

Well, without going into any shameful details, suffice it to say that if Ed McMahon doesn't come to my house with one of those big checks that'll make me scream and cry and drop to the floor of my foyer, I'm in a WHOLE lot of trouble. But at least I get to go trick-or-treating with my children in their new Tommy Hilfiger Halloween costumes. I didn't know Tommy Hilfiger even designed Halloween costumes.

Hey! Wait a minute . . . !